M000207329

Rite of Passage in the Home and Church

Raising Christ-Centered Young Adults

D. Kevin Brown

Energion Publications

www.energionpubs.com

Copyright © 2011 D. Kevin Brown

Scripture quotations are from The Holy Bible, English Standard Version, copyright © 2001 by Crossway Bibles, a division of Good News Publishers. Used by permission. All rights reserved.

Scripture quotations marked NIV are taken from the HOLY BIBLE, NEW INTERNATIONAL VERSION®, Copyright ©1973, 1978,1984 by International Bible Society. Used by permission of Zondervan Publishing House. All rights reserved.

Scripture quotations marked KJV are from the King James Version.

Cover Design: Nick May
Cover Photograph: Kevin, Katy, and Kandace Brown
Author Photograph: Michele Cordray

ISBN10: 1-893729-95-8
ISBN13: 978-1-893729-95-7
Library of Congress Control Number: 2011929271

Dedicated To:

My wife, Pam and my children, Katy, Kandace, Clara and Andrew. I'm so grateful and humbled the Lord has blessed me with you and that we have the privilege of serving Him together.

Acknowledgments

I would have never had the opportunity to write this book had it not been for Dr. David Alan Black. Dr. Black is professor of New Testament and Greek at Southeastern Baptist Theological Seminary. I have had the privilege of traveling to Ethiopia with Dr. Black and his wife, BeckyLynn. During our last trip, in the summer of 2010, Dr. Black encouraged me to write a book about my desire to teach and equip families and churches to raise Christ-centered young adults. I quickly began sharing all the reasons why I could not do so. However, over time and with some persistent prodding from Dave and my wife, I decided to take the plunge. I feel a tremendous amount of gratitude toward Dr. Black for his gentle persuasion and putting me in contact with such a great publisher. I would never have written this book if we had not met. Dave and BeckyLynn are truly my greatest spiritual mentors. I am grateful for their investment in me and family.

I want to thank Henry Neufeld, owner of Energion Publications, who helped this inexperienced writer greatly. I sincerely appreciate his time and effort in my regard. I am thankful for a publisher like Henry who gives people like me an opportunity to write a book, even though we have no prior background in the trade.

I am genuinely humbled to have such a loving church family at Mt. Pleasant Baptist Church. I appreciate immensely such a wonderful and supportive church. The many prayers and well wishes and words of encouragement during the process of writing were so inspiring. I also appreciate those dedicated men that helped teach on Wednesday nights and at Iron Men, so I could have time to write.

I learned very quickly that I needed some good proofreaders and editors to look over my shoulder and help me with grammar, spelling and content. David and Kathy Brown, my parents, along with my sister, Kim B. Church, were always ready and willing to read a stack of new material. I also want to thank Dale and Lori Jennings and Caison and Amy Jones for their insightful viewpoints and fantastic suggestions. What a blessing!

There isn't enough time or enough pages in this book to offer enough thanks to my wife, Pam, for all she did to help me in writing this book. My children endured quite a bit as well as the manuscript deadline approached and I'm thankful for their love and support. Ultimately, I could not have and would not have written this book if it had not been for their encouragement and understanding. We persevered together! I must say that Pam's help as my main proofreader was indispensable. She literally could be considered my "co-author" for this project. Her ability to express ideas and concepts is truly amazing. God knew before time began that he would pair me with an English-major. I still have in my mind the mental image of Pam lying in bed until after midnight with a red pen in hand and reading glasses on her nose feverishly editing for me. I am blessed among men!

Finally, I want to thank Jesus Christ, whom I invited into my life as a ten-year-old boy. He has patiently and lovingly been my good shepherd. He has given me an abundant life because he willingly sacrificed his own. He is my Lord and I sincerely desire to follow Him and live only for his kingdom. I am grateful that He has done immeasurably more than all I have asked or imagined according to his power that is at work within me!

Table of Contents

Foreword

I am often asked for advice from young pastors and seminarians about how to implement New Testament truth into the life of a local church. I usually refer them to members of their own generation. There are a handful of younger adults who seem to understand the church, our culture, and how to apply biblical truth to both. Writers like Eric Carpenter, Alan Knox, Arthur Sido, and Kevin Brown are people who will help the Christian community find its way forward. These men are precious gifts from God, and their contributions to the church are greatly appreciated by their blog readers. They are engaged, informed, and ready and able to offer well-reasoned and biblical responses to the issues churches face today.

How often are we wrong about our suppositions! Mary supposed Jesus was the gardener. The disciples in the boat thought He was a ghost. Joseph and Mary assumed He was traveling with them when actually He was back in Jerusalem. And how many times do we in the church assume His presence in our programs when He is nowhere to be found.

God has provided instruction on how we should raise our children. If we are to love Him with all of our heart, soul, strength, and mind, then there is a right way by which to honor Him. The heart is deceitful and desperately wicked, and so we must always go back to the Scriptures if we are to understand His ways correctly. Today we draw up our blueprints for "youth ministry" and seek divine endorsement instead of seeking first the divine Word. We do not inquire, as we should, "Lord, what do you want me to do?" It is high time we reported to His headquarters for our marching orders.

The last invitation of the Bible says, "Let the one who is thirsty come" (Rev. 22:17). My friend Kevin Brown is a pastor who hungers and thirsts desperately after God. He is conscious, deeply conscious, that there is only one source of Truth when it comes to our youth. If we drink of this Truth and receive it by faith, we will overflow to the glory of God and the blessing of others.

What a blessed pattern for youth is set forth in Scripture! Our greatest delight as parents should be to see our children living for Christ. There is indeed a biblical pattern to parenting, but there are many impediments, not least our enslavement to tradition. Our Lord was careful to stress that children were important to Him. It is a mistaken notion that youth require entertainment and games. There is no adult Holy Spirit and teenage Holy Spirit. There's just the Holy Spirit, and all who possess Christ are to love and serve Him. Paul makes this clear in 1 Corinthians 12. It is of first importance that the church stop marginalizing its youth. How ridiculous to act as though the Gospel could not transform our teenagers' lives!

You will observe that this book does not claim to be the answer to every question you might have about parenting or youth ministry. Raising responsible teenagers is a work of God. Only He can transform our lives. Except the Lord build the house we labor in vain who build it. Kevin Brown says the time for flimsy alibis is over. It will take rugged tenacity and inspired stubbornness to see it through. But the pay-off comes when the world is obliged to acknowledge that the work was performed by the Lord.

Yes, says brother Kevin, Christian young men and women can be "strong" (1 John 2:14). The tragedy of today is that our sights are too low. Have you ever considered what the Scriptures have to say about the matter? If not, I urge you to make a start of it now, by reading this excellent book. Our Father would be pleased to give us so much more if we only had the faith to ask for it.

David Alan Black
Professor of New Testament and Greek
Southeastern Baptist Theological Seminary

Preface

I am excited about the fact that this is my first book. Writing it was something I greatly enjoyed. Yet at times I found it to be completely overwhelming. About half-way into the book I had one of those "What have you done?" moments. But, obviously you are holding the finished product indicating the Lord guided and blessed me through it. I must say that I was exceedingly stretched in this process. I'm not afraid of being stretched, but I was pulled spiritually and emotionally in ways I have never been. I'm grateful for that stretching and how the Lord has used it to mold me into a more surrendered disciple. My family was stretched right along with me and I'm thankful they were so supportive through it all.

I realized in writing this book that I am a complete and utter failure without Jesus Christ. I am incapable of imparting any worthwhile knowledge to anyone that is worthwhile apart from the grace of God. After all, I have not even finished raising my own children. How can I possibly have anything to say to anyone who is in the process of raising or training children in some capacity? Yet I can write this book, not because of anything I have done or am doing. I have no great wisdom and claim no authority, except that of the Holy Scriptures.

I am a pastor at Mt. Pleasant Baptist Church (MPBC) in Wilkesboro, NC. Wilkesboro is located in the foothills of the Blue Ridge Mountains. Here is the amazing thing that astounds most people. I was literally raised in the church that I now pastor. I have been at MPBC since I was a one-year-old. I was chosen by the church body from within the ranks of the church family. We see this example in the book of Acts. Paul appointed elders in this manner, so I was not parachuted in; instead I was home-grown!

I was a businessman, mainly in the areas of finance and sales, for over 17 years before sensing the desire and leading from the

Lord to shepherd his people. I'm still overwhelmed he manifested this desire and orchestrated the circumstances for them to be fulfilled in my home church. I have a passion for teaching and discipling men and families. I also have a strong desire for equipping the church for works of service. This passion for teaching has led me to the writing of this book.

I would like to tell you a little bit about my family. Most books only give a passing glance about the author and his or her background. Often, this leaves one to wonder about the author and his or her perspective. I thought I'd share a few things about my family, because this book is about a family subject written by a family man. Here is a picture of the Browns:

Kandace, Kevin, Clara, Andrew, Pam and Katy

I am blessed to be married to a most wonderful and dedicated wife, Pam. She is indeed my suitable helper. She truly is my best friend and confidant. Pam was an English-major in college and her editing skills were put to the test with this book. Pam also has a Master's Degree in elementary education. We have been married 20 years and we are the parents of four children. Katy is 17, Kandace is 13, and Clara and Andrew are 6. We adopted Clara and Andrew from China.

Katy loves reading, writing, blogging and playing several instruments (piano, guitar and viola). Katy also sings and plays in our church praise team. Kandace enjoys reading, clogging and playing the violin and mandolin. She assists teaching ballet at a local dance studio and also sings in the ladies' ensemble at church. Both ladies are tremendous blessings and provide great help with Clara and Andrew. Clara loves music, ballet and singing. She's constantly performing her ballet leaps around the house! Andrew is our little engineer. He enjoys building with anything he can stack, bundle or pile. He adores his sisters, and yes, they spoil him!

Writing this book has truly been a labor of love. It has been written to express my heart-felt desire to disciple Christ-centered young adults. The Christian faith depends upon the transfer of the gospel from one generation to the next. This book chronicles and describes the scriptural process for accomplishing this goal. I sincerely hope you enjoy reading this book and I pray it will challenge, encourage and inspire you as well.

1

Houston, We Have a Problem

APOLLO 13

Even if you aren't totally familiar with the 1970 voyage of Apollo 13, you are probably familiar with the expression made famous by astronaut Jim Lovell, "Houston, we have a problem." Jim Lovell shared these now infamous words as he and two other flight partners, Fred Haise and Jack Swigert, learned that the explosion of an onboard-oxygen tank had crippled their spacecraft. Perhaps some of you may remember this event that took place on April 13, 1970. Some may have even watched this drama unfold on TV. I was only 2-years-old and can't remember it at all; but I have seen the 1995 movie directed by Ron Howard, starring Tom Hanks. The movie documents how hundreds of people in the Houston Texas Mission Control Center worked to bring these men home. For those of you who know the story or have seen the movie, you know the breathtaking adventure that it was for these three astronauts, their families and the American public. It seems those who were around in 1970 were glued to their TV as they wondered, prayed and hoped that somehow these men could be rescued and brought safely home.

Imagine this scene with me. Put yourself back into 1970. You have just heard about the explosion in space. Everyone is wondering what is going to happen to these three astronauts in that tiny little capsule. Could the experts at Houston's Mission Control get them home? The crippled capsule is called the *Odyssey* and it is hurtling through space headed toward the earth's atmosphere at 35,245 feet per second. The astronauts are losing oxygen. All the computers on board the *Odyssey* are basically unusable because of the explosion. Mission Control has to figure out a way to slingshot the spaceship around the moon and back into earth's atmosphere. Without computer guidance, the prospects of doing so seem impossible. Everyone is told there are no guarantees and the *Odyssey* could miss the earth completely or bounce off the atmosphere, if they do not hit it at the right trajectory. The heat shield on the underbelly of the *Odyssey*, which protects the men from the blazing inferno on reentry, may be cracked and they could burn up. Even if they make it through the earth's atmosphere, the parachutes may not open upon reentry.

The famous and reliable, CBS News anchorman, Walter Cronkite is giving play by play of these events. There are TV cameras on board the *USS Iwo Jima* in the South Pacific, where the *Odyssey* is supposed to hit the ocean upon reentry. The world waits. Everyone has been told the ordeal of reentry to our atmosphere will last several minutes. There will be radio silence, or blackout, during *Odyssey's* superheated reentry through the earth's atmosphere. Walter Cronkite reports, "With no radio signal, there will be no way to tell how the crew and ship are faring." Astronaut Jim Lovell radios to Mission Control they are preparing to make reentry. Then there is silence. Nothing but the static of the radio can be heard in Houston and across America by way of television. Cronkite indicates the blackout should last three minutes.

Time inches forward, second by second. People look at their watches or mantle clocks as the seconds tick off, counting down the time. Finally three minutes elapse and Houston makes the radio call, "*Odyssey*, this is Houston, do you read me?" This radio request is repeated over and over again. Cronkite alerts the waiting world, "Expected time of reacquisition, the time when the astronauts were expected to come out of blackout, has come and gone." Cronkite continues with a shaky and uncertain voice, "About all we can do now is just listen, and … hope." "*Odyssey* this is Houston, do you read me?" comes the request again from Mission Control. Three minutes and thirty seconds have now elapsed. "*Odyssey* this is Houston, do you copy?" A flight engineer from Mission Control breaks in, "That's four minutes … standing by." The spaceship is now one minute beyond the maximum. All hope seems lost. Again the request is made, "*Odyssey,* this is Houston. Do you read me? Come in please!"

What happens next would send goose bumps over the arm of even the most hardened person. On the TV screen appear three small, red parachutes above the blackened, silvery spacecraft dangling below. Suddenly, through the static of the radio, everyone hears these words, "Uh, Hello Houston, this is *Odyssey*. It's good to see you again!" The engineers, scientists and experts at Mission Control and literally all of America explode in spontaneous cheering and clapping! Tears flow uncontrollably even from Walter Cronkite, who removes his black, horn-rimmed glasses to wipe his cheek. The cheering, hugs, kisses, tears and joy flow in tumultuous jubilation! They made it! They made it! Thank God they made it home!

I've watched that movie and that scene at least a dozen times through the years and even in writing the last paragraph there are tears in my eyes. It's emotional! Against almost all odds these three men made it home safely! "Welcome home!" they were told by Mission Control in Houston. When I think about the total relief that must have flooded the minds and hearts of the families and all the friends of the astronauts, it is awe-inspiring to me. They made it back home! They are alive, safe and sound!

Our Problem

I share this extended account of the journey of Apollo 13 to the moon because it parallels what I would like to share with you in this book. Apollo 13 and its voyage to the moon is analogous to the journey of raising and training young adults. It is a journey filled with many difficulties and uncertainties. Much like the training of astronauts, we are training our children or young people in an attempt to one day catapult them into adulthood. I'm not talking about just raising young adults for the sake of saying they are grown; rather, I'm talking about raising Christ-centered young adults. If that is a goal for you and your family, or for you and your ministry, then we must realize something. Many are sending their children off to college, work and adulthood, just as rockets sent the *Odyssey* to the moon. The mission of Apollo 13 was to land on to the moon, yet they didn't make it. Many of our children aren't reaching their destination. What is that destination? Christ-centered adulthood is their mission, yet many of our young people are not developing into Christ-centered young adults. Therefore, we must sound the alarm and declare, "Houston, we have a problem."

There are no magic potions or sure-fire methods that can guarantee the mission of producing young adults who will be Christ-centered and rock-solid in their faith. Yet, I am convinced there are Scriptural patterns, if heeded, which can give us greater confidence toward accomplishing our mission. The purpose of this book is to share what I believe are those patterns and how we can implement them in our homes and churches.

After being a business man for many years, I realized God was moving me toward and giving me a desire to become a pastor. Initially, I served in an associate pastor role, yet, I was viewed by most as the "youth pastor." Later I became the pastor of this same church and it's where I continue to pastor today. Prior to sensing God's prompting me to be recognized as an elder/pastor, I had taught the high school Sunday School class for 17 years. I saw first-hand and had become very dismayed by the exodus of our young adults from the church soon after graduation. I saw this abandonment was not just taking place at the church I attended and helped to lead, but was, and is, taking place in many churches throughout the nation across all denominations.

I consider it unfortunate that I have first-hand experience of this exodus. Yet, because of my many years of teaching and subsequently having seen many young adults walk away from the church and ultimately the faith, I began to seek answers to this troubling dilemma. At this point I want you to know that I in no way intend to come across as one having all the answers. I don't want to give even the slightest impression that I have even most of the answers. The truth is that my family and I are still a "work in progress." I struggle every day as a parent. Being a parent is the hardest thing I've ever done. Yet, I believe through the many years of being in the trenches, I have learned some things that may warrant consideration.

In America today, we have a problem in Christendom. Our young people are graduating from our high schools and heading off to work or college and are subsequently walking away from their faith. Simply put, we are not accomplishing the mission of making disciples. Jesus said that we are to go and make disciples of all nations (see Matt. 28:19-20). But, we are making very few. Indeed we should say, "Houston, we have a problem!" Statistics show we are failing miserably in producing godly young adults that continue or remain in their faith (see barna.org for many of these studies and statistical analysis.) To use the failed Apollo 13 mission to describe our families, there has been an "explosion" onboard and now we must figure out a way to get our young people safely home. I'm not talking about the home where they grew up; instead, I'm talking about the home in heaven that awaits the genuine believer in Christ. We must change our mindsets, course of action and ultimately our ecclesiology. If we don't, we stand to lose an entire generation of young adults; if this hasn't already happened right under our noses, not to mention subsequent generations.

We must come to grips with the truth that stares us in the face. We must admit that we have a problem. Many have become comfortable with simply dropping their kids off at church and claiming "Train up a child in the way he should go: and when he is old, he will not depart from it" (Prov. 22:6 KJV). Yet, we will come to understand this modern-day pattern is not Scriptural and is an utter failure. The problem of our young people walking away is centered in a problem that is in our homes, not our churches.

WHAT'S GOING ON?

To illustrate this problem, consider what is happening in many "Christian" homes today. A child or young person is disrespectful and dishonoring in their actions and their speech. They have little or no desire for the things of God and they have to be coaxed, begged or bribed to attend church. They struggle mightily in how they speak to you as their parent and their siblings. Their speech is often rude, unkind or mean. Yet, they claim to be a Christian. If this is the case, can you see there has been an "explosion" onboard? Should we be entrusting their eternity in their profession of faith in Christ if this is the behavior we are witnessing? Could it be that what we are seeing evidenced in their lives is the absence of the Holy Spirit of God? Some would say, "No, it's just immaturity." I understand that conclusion. But the Bible says, "Even a child makes himself known by his acts, by whether his conduct is pure and upright" (Prov. 20:11). Could it be that their behavior is revealing the truth of who they really are? Would we want to swallow hard and admit that their selfishness, irresponsibility and lack of godliness are quite simply indications that they are a sinner? After all, isn't this how a "sinner" behaves?

I understand what I've described might not be indicative of your situation, but do you know homes like this? What I will describe in this book has *everything* to do with the work of the Holy Spirit of God and *very little* to do with some new approach or program.

I will attempt to define the patterns of raising Christ-centered young adults through a process I call "Rite of Passage" (ROP). From the beginning, I want you to understand ROP is not something new. It is actually something as old as Scripture. It is a process of teaching, admonishing and training our young people that brings with it specific expectations and encouragements that work within families and between families in the Body of Christ.

ROP exposes parents and children to what the Bible teaches about becoming and acting like a young adult. ROP has become a high water mark for many young people in the church I help to lead. In fact the children in our church can't wait to turn 12 and be eligible, upon parental approval, for participation in this spiritual process. I describe ROP in detail in chapter 5, but I want you to understand at this point that ROP is simply a process that mirrors Scripture in training our young people. ROP has as its ultimate goal the statement of Christ as a 12-year-old: "Didn't you know I had to be about my Father's business?" ROP is much more than just another program that you have in your church or in your home. It's also *not* a quick-hit program that one uses at the end of the child's upbringing. ROP is truly a way of life or the ultimate mission of a family that begins when the children are born. It is a way of describing the spiritual nature and process of the training and admonition which must take place on a daily basis so that our children may have an opportunity to truly understand what it means to *live* for Jesus Christ as their Lord. This process must be 100% Spirit-led and Spirit-guided. The Spirit of God is our "mission control." Ultimately, ROP is the culmination of years of teaching and training in the home with the church assisting and helping to acknowledge and applaud those dedicated efforts to raise Christian young adults.

FINDING OUR WAY BACK

I am totally convinced the answer to our problem regarding the exodus, en masse, of our young adults lies in the pages of Scripture. We must return to the ancient paths as detailed in the Word of God. In so doing, we will find answers, instructions and many admonitions on how to successfully complete our mission. We will come to understand it is not the job of the church to spiritually raise children for parents. It is not my job, as a church leader, nor the job of the church to do for the family what God has designed as the work of the family. My job, and that of the church, is to work *with* the family in order to help encourage dads and moms in the process of raising and training Christ-centered young adults in their homes.

As church leaders, we must sincerely look at our efforts as churches regarding the effectiveness of our programs and analyze the return on investment we have been reaping. We must determine if these programs and the massive expenditures that go with them are worthwhile. I hope to show the ultimate program should be designed to partner with parents, particularly fathers in teaching and training their children (see Eph. 6:1-4). I am well aware that what I share could, at times, be considered somewhat controversial. However, Scripture and its principles are always counter-cultural. At times, I sincerely feel like a "voice crying out in the wilderness." I know the teaching contained in the pages of this book will truly require a paradigm shift and for some, may even cause the proverbial bone to stick in the throat. Why do I say this? It may be hard to hear, but even those of us in the church have a great tendency to follow the crowd. After all, we say, "Everyone is doing church this way." As we know, just because everyone is doing it, doesn't make the method right. Being different, even if we learn it is Biblical, scares most people and it can certainly be intimidating to make tough choices.

Truthfully, what we have been doing over the last 30-40 years in our homes and churches is simply *not* working and we are losing another generation of young people. I hope to show how ROP can be a conduit through which the church and primarily the families of our young adults can successfully bring our children home, even when there is a period of silence and all we seem to hear is radio static. In the pages of this book, we will learn about a "Rite of Passage" way of living that will help us to clarify what are *essentials* in raising genuinely committed Christ-followers.

After the crippled *Odyssey* sent the radio message back to earth, "Houston, we have a problem," Mission Control worked tirelessly to get the little command module back home. The engineers and scientists studied and diligently dissected the manuals of each piece of equipment that was onboard that spaceship. They found within the pages of those manuals a way to keep the three men alive until they could figure out how to get them back home. We too, have a manual, the Bible. We, as parents are the engineers at mission control in our homes. We have the responsibility of getting our children and young adults safely home. We must look to that great manual of life to find the answers. To the degree we read Scripture, study it, heed it, and follow it, will determine the degree of success we will have in making prudent and wise decisions in any area of life. ROP will help us to identify these Scriptural reference points, by which we must navigate our children, if we want to get them safely home. That's our mission, and in the words of Gene Kranz, the Flight Director for Mission Control in 1970, "Failure is not an option!"

2

Rite of Passage (ROP)-
What Is It and
Why Do We Need It?

THE CRUX OF THE MATTER

If you are reading this book, then you are probably like me; you care about young people. Whether you are a parent and the children happen to be your own or you are in a position of leadership in your church, the common denominator of those reading this book are the children and young people in our lives. After all, we want to raise Christ-centered young adults. We desire to train and equip young people so that as adults, they are grounded in the faith and are truly followers of Jesus Christ. Certainly, this is a worthy goal and one that, if attained, will come at a price.

For seventeen years I had the privilege of teaching a high school Sunday school class in the church I now pastor. During those years, I watched young people come and go. The class age range was 7th grade through 12th grade. Obviously, this was a challenging class to teach because of the wide range of ages. However, the Lord blessed and I enjoyed those many years of teaching. Yet, after about 15 years of instructing, I began to notice something. As the young adults graduated from my class and moved on to college or a career, I recognized that many of these former students were strikingly "missing in action." As I talked to other parents and people that worked with young people, they were telling me the same thing.

I decided to go back through my printed Sunday school "attendance rolls" and I perused the names of the young adults I had taught over those 17 years. As I did, I began thinking about the students and where they were and what they were doing. After completing that task, it struck me that around 80% of those that I had taught were no longer in church at all. Shortly after that, I began hearing about more and more studies that showed the same thing among young adults within mainline and evangelical churches. These studies (depending upon the one you choose to read, because there are many) showed that between 70% and 92% of "Christian" teens were dropping out of church and abandoning their faith, most by their 20th birthday (see barna.org). As I saw these statistics playing out in my own church setting, I became alarmed! What in the world is going on? Why are we losing so many of our young people? What is happening to them? Why are they walking away?

I began a process of intense prayer and Scripture study. I also began reading everything I could get my hands on to try to help me understand why we were failing to keep our young adults engaged in Christianity and in church. What I discovered left my head spinning. We are failing—miserably! That was and is the bottom line. We, as Christian parents and as mainline and evangelical churches, are failing to pass the baton of our faith in Jesus Christ to our children. Why?

There are so many reasons that could be explored and while many are worthy of our time, I want to share with you what I believe is the crux of the matter. Before I do, I would like to say this to you, the reader. You may or may not agree with what I'm about to share with you, but if you will look at the research, study the Scriptures and seek the Lord in prayer, I believe you will discover that there is truth and validity in my premise.

So, what is the problem? Why are we losing our young people in droves? Why are they walking away from the church and their faith en masse? *We aren't raising disciples of Jesus Christ.* That's right! Although this is obviously not intentional, the truth is we are not raising *genuine disciples of Christ*. When it comes to their children's faith, many parents seem to think if they drop them off at church and the child eventually makes a profession of faith, then their job is done.

We must honestly admit there are young people growing up in "Christian" homes and in our churches who are not truly followers of Jesus Christ. How can we tell? They leave home and never return to Christ. They remain "missing in action." They made a decision as a child, we call it "getting saved"; but where are they now? Perhaps you can look at your own congregation or family and see this same pattern.

We are implored by the psalmist in Psalm 78:6-7 to teach our children:

> ... *that the next generation might know them, the children yet unborn, and arise and tell them to their children, so that they should set their hope in God and not forget the works of God, but keep his commandments ...*

Many "Christian teens" who have grown up in our churches and in our children and youth programs know (in their heads) all about Jesus. They know he is the son of God who died for their sins. They know he rose from the dead and sits at the right hand of God in heaven today. The problem is, or should I say the crux of the matter is, this basic, elementary knowledge is where their faith and commitment appear to end. Yes, it seems their spiritual growth just stops for most children after they "pray to receive Jesus into their lives." Consequently, I've become convinced, after watching this process for the majority of my life, that many young adults have only a basic knowledge of Jesus Christ and his teachings. As a dear brother in Christ of mine says, "It seems they have the spiritual depth of a mud puddle." Are we possibly just replicating what *we are* ourselves? I am speaking here of the church in America as a whole. Sadly, many Christians are spiritually anemic with little Bible knowledge and with even less desire to "die to self" and "take up their cross daily."

Perhaps as you are reading, you are beginning to wonder: *Are the 70-92% who leave the faith unsaved or just spiritually anemic?* That is a critical question isn't it? But we're not ready to tackle that question full throttle just yet. If I may ask for your patience, we will return to this question later in the chapter.

For now, it is clear we have many good desires for our young adults. We want them to grow up and be healthy, smart, well-adjusted and most of all (for many it seems) well-educated young adults. So, we push them toward education. I believe we have in many instances made education a god in America. The goals for many Christian families are the same as those of the world. We want our kids to pursue making money and living comfortably, "happily ever after." Consequently, with these life pursuits as their goals, they grow up having little, if any, spiritual depth. Understandably, with no clear spiritual goals, this will almost certainly be the outcome. Is this what we really want? Of course it isn't, or at least I hope not. I distinctly remember Jesus saying that it profits a man nothing if he gains the whole world, yet loses his own soul (Matt. 16:26). So, how has this happened to us?

THE CULTURE OF THE "KIDULT"

Let me ask this question. Do we in our culture, even in our Christian homes, really expect much from our young adults? Many parents have high expectations in some areas such as academics or athletics. Maybe we could look at it this way: From whom do we expect more, a toddler or a teenager? Now really think about that for a moment. Why do toddlers, with inferior motor skills, reasoning ability, and physical strength, experience nearly 100% success in overcoming difficult challenges as they grow, while teens falter? Maybe it's because toddlers are expected to mature and teenagers aren't. Does that sound harsh? Think about it. We expect toddlers to grow up, but for some reason, not our teens. We almost expect teenagers to go into some sort of dormant state of maturity in their teen years. We even expect this among our Christian teenagers. Once they become teenagers, many it seems get a free pass until they graduate from college or perhaps even longer. I'm convinced there has developed in our culture today what are called "kidults."

Are you curious about that word: kidult? What is a "kidult?" That word has been used to describe a growing group of young adults in our nation. They are adults who have never grown up and still act like kids. Hence we have the name, "kidult." I first saw this name used in a *Time* magazine article entitled "Grow Up? Not so Fast" (*Time* 2005). Grossman described kidults in the article this way:

> Everybody knows a few of them—full-grown men and women who still live with their parents, who dress and talk and party as they did in their teens, hopping from job to job and date to date, having fun but seemingly going nowhere.

Kidults generally have no clear direction or a sense of urgency about anything. Legally they are adults, but they are still acting like kids. They are on the threshold of adulthood, but refuse to walk through the door. They're standing at the end of the diving board, but they refuse to jump in. The Bible says in 1 Corinthians 14:20: "Brothers, stop thinking like children. In regard to evil be infants, but in your thinking be adults." I remember thinking as I read the article, "This describes so many young adults today, but why have we accepted this unbiblical viewpoint?" Has this kidult worldview permeated our thinking as believers too? Are we raising kidults? Could this possibly be contributing to why so many of our young people walk away from their faith?

THE MYTH OF ADOLESCENCE

As I contemplated the article and continued to seek answers, I was introduced to a book written by Dr. David Alan Black, professor of Greek and New Testament at Southeastern Baptist Theological Seminary. his book is titled: *The Myth of Adolescence: Raising Responsible Children in an Irresponsible Society.* While reading, I realized there were things I knew intuitively that was a paradigm shift for me. Beliefs I held about raising children and even ministry to youth were beginning to change. I want to be clear. Dr. Black's book opened my eyes to passages of Scripture that I knew, but had not connected the dots regarding children and adults. As I continued to read, pray, study, and seek answers, it hit me. I had adopted a humanistic belief system that says there is some sort of "in between" time for our young adults. However, the Bible teaches nothing of the sort.

In our western culture we often raise our young adults and send them off to college. There they live in an extended period of adolescent revelry of which they have a very difficult time growing out of, even as 30-somethings. But, let's think about it, why should they grow up? What is it in our culture and society that's out there in the real world to tell them it's time to grow up? Is it when they get a driver's license at the age of 16? Is it when they graduate from high school, serve in the military, or can vote at age 18? Is it when they can buy liquor at age 21? Is it when they graduate from college? Is it when they get married or have children? When is it?

There seems to be no clear mile marker for our young people today. Therefore, many meander in a hazy twilight between childhood and adulthood. Dr. Black sums up the dilemma in his book (Black 1999, 85):

> Mass confusion reigns among our teens. … Because our society has no rite of adulthood, today's young people often look to other self-defined rites of passage. They are desperate for some way to prove themselves and others that they are no longer children. Some teens see the use of alcohol, tobacco, or drugs as an introduction into adulthood. Others believe having sexual intercourse or breaking a law makes them adults. Still others turn to peer groups, including gangs, for their identity. Even if the group is 'good' (such as a church youth group), when the

group breaks up, the teen is again left without an identity.

When I read that paragraph I said, "That's it! He's right!" There is not a mile marker or *rite of passage* for our young adults, even in our church youth groups. Not only do young people not know when to grow up, neither do their parents. I was no different. I wasn't exactly sure when to expect adult behaviors and attitudes from my own children.

What I began to realize is we need a way to move our children from being "child-like" to becoming young adults with desires and responsibilities that are more godly and mature. Is this possible? Can we expect teenagers to act like "adults?" Isn't this unrealistic? For example, how many 15-year-olds do you know who are acting like and living like a young adult? My guess is you won't be able to think of more than a handful. Why? Because, we don't know when to expect them to act like a young adult.

At this point, I believe it's important for us to look at and understand this period of time in the life of a young person we call a teenager or an adolescent. We must do so in order to understand where we are as a culture today. Only in the last 75-80 years has the term "adolescence" or "adolescent" been used. From the beginning of time on this earth until just after World War II, there were two groups of people: children and adults. You became an adult when you could plow the fields as a young man or as a young lady you could take care of your siblings. Certainly we do not live in an agrarian society today. However, because of this fact, we no longer seem to have a way of determining when a young person is supposed to be grown up.

Over time we have bought into the premise that teenagers are to be granted a season of life where they can sow their wild oats, be lazy, disrespectful, messy, irresponsible, and have little or no motivation to do much of anything except to sleep, eat and go to school. Is this acceptable? Should we resign ourselves to the fact that when a person turns 13, he or she is going to "check out" on the world for years and years? Surely not! That brings us back to the purpose of this book. When do we expect them to grow up and what can we do to get them there?

The scientific community has much to say about adolescence. I could give you quote after quote from leading child psychologists, therapists and doctors from across the world about their theories on adolescence. I could give you their perspective in detail and we could dive into their "worldview," dissecting the topic of adolescence from a myriad of clinical angles. But, I won't. Why? Because I'm more interested in discovering what the Scriptures teach. Don't get me wrong. I'm not saying we shouldn't read, study, and listen to what psychologists, therapists and doctors have to say, but listening to them exclusively or even primarily speak seems to be a large part of the problem. I believe we have neglected the instruction and admonition of the Bible for far too long. What if we were to use Scripture as our compass and guide?

SOLA SCRIPTURA

The phrase *sola scriptura* is from the Latin: *sola* having the idea of "alone," "ground," "base," and the word *scriptura* meaning "writings"—referring to the Scriptures. *Sola scriptura* means that Scripture alone is authoritative for the faith and practice of the Christian. The Bible is complete, authoritative, and true. The Bible declares itself to be God-breathed, inerrant and authoritative. We know God does not change his mind or contradict himself. The Bible is not bound by time; instead it is timeless. So, while the Bible itself may not explicitly argue for *sola scriptura*, it most definitely does not allow for traditions that contradict its message. *Sola scriptura* is not as much of an argument against tradition as it is an argument against unbiblical, extra-biblical and/or anti-biblical doctrines. The only way to know for sure what God expects of us is to stay true to what we know he has revealed—the Bible. We can know, beyond the shadow of any doubt, that Scripture is true, authoritative and reliable. The same cannot be said of tradition or the wisdom of man.

The Word of God is the only authority for the Christian faith. However, in the church it is so easy to look to our traditions and the way we do things as being right. Yet, traditions or man's ways are valid only when they are based on Scripture and are in full agreement with Scripture. Traditions that contradict the Bible are not of God and are not a valid aspect of the Christian faith. Sola scriptura is the only way to avoid subjectivity and keep personal opinion from taking priority over the teachings of the Bible. The essence of sola scriptura is basing your spiritual life on the Bible alone and rejecting any tradition or teaching that is not in full agreement with the Bible. Paul told Timothy in 2 Timothy 2:15, "Do your best to present yourself to God as one approved, a worker who has no need to be ashamed, rightly handling the word of truth."

Sola scriptura does not nullify the concept of church traditions and our current practices within our churches. Rather, *sola scriptura* gives us a solid foundation on which to test and analyze our traditions and practices. There are many practices in our churches that are the result of traditions and not the explicit teaching of Scripture. Please don't misunderstand; it is good, and even necessary, for the church to have traditions. Traditions play an important role in clarifying and organizing Christian practice. At the same time, in order for these traditions to be valid, they must not be in disagreement with God's Word. They must be based on the solid foundation of the teaching of Scripture.

Isn't this an interesting thought? Using the Bible to govern our lives and dictate our actions seems almost novel in our culture? We have so many competing voices giving us instruction and direction. There are talk show hosts, advice columnists and experts of all kinds telling us how to raise and instruct our children. Who needs the Bible? Whether we would like to admit it or not, it's easy to call yourself a Christian in our culture and never pick up a Bible. Sadly, many believers listen to anybody and everybody, but seldom turn to the Scriptures for guidance. In our case, I want to ask you to take what I call the "Sola Scriptura Challenge" with me. I want you to imagine that all we have to govern our lives and give us insight and direction is the Word of God. I want you to imagine that we are going to *literally* follow the teaching of Psalm 119:105

> *Your word is a lamp for my feet, a light on my path.*

From this point forward, we are going to throw out all other worldviews we may have, except what we see through the lens of Scripture. In other words, the worldview (our overall perspective from which we see and interpret the world and life) will be based on Scripture alone. We will exclusively use Scripture to teach us how we are to raise Christ-centered, young adults. Why? Why should we use anything but Scripture? Let's think about it. The Word of God is supernatural. It's *alive* and *active*. It is described in Hebrews 4:12 as being as sharp as a double-edged sword. It can divide and penetrate soul and spirit, as well as the thoughts and attitudes of the heart. The Word of God is indeed the most powerful, tangible object in the universe. It's better than dynamite to blow up our misconceptions and preconceived notions that have been subversively planted in our brains by the world system in which we're immersed. When it comes to looking for answers as to *how* to effectively train Christ-centered, young adults, I will look to Scripture alone. I will seek to give a word from the Word. Are you with me? Would you be willing to take the "Solo Scriptura Challenge" with me?

If you will take this challenge, I promise you will indeed be challenged and you will, at times, be scratching your head and saying, "What?" There will be occasions when you say, "I don't agree at all with what he is saying!" In fact, I'm going to tell you here and now that there are things that I'm still wrestling with in my own life and in my own mind that the Scriptures are helping me to understand. I have a western education in which I was "raised" in public schools and a public university. Therefore, I'm certain my worldview is still tainted because of the secular, evolutionary teaching I received. However, I am growing as I read and study the Bible. In fact, I can look back over my life, even just ten years ago and say, "Wow! Did I really believe that back then?"

Therefore, please understand that I'm a work in progress. I don't have all the answers, nor do I claim to have even most of the answers. However, the Word of God does have all the answers. We simply have to dig them out, as looking for buried treasure.

WHAT DOES THE BIBLE SAY ABOUT ADOLESCENCE?

What do the Scriptures say about adolescence? I sense a paradigm shift in our thinking may be coming. The Scriptures say nothing about adolescence. Not a word! Let me state that again. The Bible says absolutely *zero* about adolescence. Are you surprised? Isn't it funny how there are things you might expect to find in Scripture which simply aren't there? It's true. You can look through the entire Bible and you'll never find a single reference in Scripture regarding an *adolescent* or *adolescence*. What you will find in Scripture is that people went directly from childhood to adulthood. Study the Old Testament and you will find the Hebrews never acknowledge a period or season of adolescence among God's people.

In the New Testament, the apostle Paul tells us in 1 Corinthians 13:11, "When I was a child, I spoke like a child, I thought like a child, I reasoned like a child. When I became a man, I gave up childish ways." The word "adolescence" is not found in that passage or in any other New Testament passage. Paul shows us the Scriptural pattern of change when we go from being a child to a man. He notes three specific things: language, thinking and reasoning. Certainly this is true, for one can tell if someone is a child rather than a man or woman by how he or she talks, thinks and reasons.

Paul expresses this concept in even greater detail to young Timothy, whom many scholars say was a young man, most likely in his teens, in 1 Timothy 4:12:

> *Let no one despise you for your youth, but set the believers an example in speech, in conduct, in love, in faith, in purity.*

I'll expound more about Timothy later in the chapter when we discuss Scriptural models, but at this point, we can see the Bible makes a direct, non-stop flight from "child to adult" with no stopovers at a place called "adolescence."

HELL INSURANCE

Surveys on young adults reveal all kinds of interesting information. However, this information is more than just interesting to me. It goes much deeper than that. As I read the statistics of how our young adults are disinterested and disengaged in the things of God, it concerned me, creating deeper fears and concerns in my spirit. Let me give you a brief example. David Kinnaman, president of the Barna Research Group (barna.org. 2006) cited:

> For most adults, this pattern of disengagement is not merely a temporary phase in which they test the boundaries of independence, but is one that continues deeper into adulthood, with those in their thirties also less likely than older adults to be religiously active. Even the traditional impulse of parenthood - when people's desire to supply spiritual guidance for their children pulls them back to church - is weakening.

Although I share the information with you from this study, I don't think we are seeing the full picture. However it is not Kinnaman's or Barna's fault. There is something going on here that may not initially meet the eye. Nonetheless, it is critical to our understanding of what is happening to our young people and why they appear to be walking away from their faith. As a father of four children and as an elder/pastor, what I will share with you concerns me more than almost anything else. My concern is that the statisticians, unknowingly, may have it all wrong when it comes to their surveys and statistics. I believe the research that is being done today and in the past few years regarding young adults and their faith has potentially a faulty premise. What is that potentially faulty premise? The researchers are taking the young adults' word that they are Christians. Certainly, the researchers ask them in various ways, if they are "saved" or a "believer" in Christ. They record these answers and move forward with their surveys.

Here's the problem. The researchers and statisticians must take the young adult's word that they are truly a believer in Christ. They don't have time to really try to determine if this is genuinely true or not. In fact, this is something you can't discover in an interview over the phone or from the internet. Why do I bring this up? I bring it up because I'm very concerned that many of our young people who *claim* to be Christians (saved) might not be at all. Let me be clear. I'm not implying that our teenagers are lying. I'm simply stating that what they say might not match with what is *true* in their lives. In fact, they might not truly know the difference.

Let's probe a little deeper. As I have indicated, based on whatever research you may want to quote or site, approximately 70%-92% of teenagers will walk away from their faith and abandon the church within a few years after high school graduation. Those statistics alone keep me up at night. But, it is what's behind the numbers that concerns me the most. Behind those statistics are young people who may not know Jesus Christ as their Lord. Let's be honest, for most of us, it's not hard, nor will it get us into trouble, to admit that we are a Christian. In fact, if you live in the south, where I do, it's expected. Seriously, a young person in our southern churches is expected to "ask Jesus into their heart" by the time they are a teenager. If they don't, then most people would say something is wrong. Is this a good thing? Maybe it is and maybe it isn't.

I want you to consider something for a moment. How many children do you see being led to Christ in the New Testament? Can you think of any? I can't. Yet, Jesus said to let the little children come to him. He said we must have a *child-like* faith to enter the kingdom. Certainly this is true. We must come trusting, as a child trusts and has faith in a parent, when we come to Christ. But here is my point. It seems that Jesus and the apostles focused on discipling the adults (those over 12 years of age). Outside of the instance when Jesus scolded the disciples for not letting the children come to him, all of Jesus' encounters that we are privy to in Scripture were with people 12 years of age or older.

Why do I make this point? Simply because I believe for many followers of Christ today, including myself, there was a time that we prayed to receive Jesus into our lives as a child because we were scared of going to Hell. Certainly there are other reasons a child may pray to receive Christ in their lives, but most of the children and adults I know, prayed to receive Christ because of their fear of Hell. Yet, for many Christians who "prayed a prayer" as a child; there was a time later in life, when they made the choice to allow Jesus to be the "Lord" or boss of their life. Does this scenario describe your personal experience? Many people want Jesus as Savior, because they truly don't want to go to Hell. But, at some point in our lives, he must become more than "Hell insurance." The Bible says that one day every knee will bow and every tongue confess that he is Lord, not just "Savior." We will confess he is "Lord." The semantics are important here. Scripture teaches in the book of Romans that if we confess with our mouths that "Jesus is Lord," it will lead the heart to righteous living. That means we will live right. Why? Because Jesus is Lord!

Children typically pray to receive Christ in their lives when they are very young. Often this takes place in Vacation Bible School, a Sunday school class, during a church service, or possibly at a special event, such as a youth camp/retreat, revival, concert, or crusade. Certainly, what I've described doesn't cover it all, but you get the point. Now the question is: *Did they sincerely and genuinely become a follower of Jesus Christ?* Were they regenerated? Did old things pass away and all things become new? Did they truly become a new creation?

At this point we may say, "Well, we are just going to have to take their word for it." This is exactly what researchers, many in the church, and even we have done in our own homes. We have taken their word for it. But, this is not how Jesus did it. He said, "These people honor me with their lips, but their heart is far from me" (Matt. 15:8). Jesus said, "Thus you will recognize them by their fruits" (Matt. 7:20). Jesus looked at what a person did, not what they said. Jesus said, "If you love me, you will keep my commands" (John 14:15). If we love Jesus, we *will* (not might) keep his commands. I'm not implying we will be perfect, but we should be exhibiting evidence that we're a new creation. Therefore, if we are using Scripture as our guide, we should notice *fruit*. I'm referring to the fruit of the Spirit (see Gal. 5:22-23). We are not judging, as some would accuse. Rather, we are looking for evidence of a genuine walk with Christ. We are "fruit inspectors."

I have had the privilege to travel to Ethiopia to do mission work. In southern Ethiopia there are plants or trees called inset trees. These trees look exactly like banana trees. Their leaves look identical to a banana tree, but the difference is the inset tree grows no bananas. The inset tree is commonly called the "false banana" tree. Could this be true of many Christians? Could it be true of our teens? Could they look like Christians and give outward indication they are a Christian, but give little or no evidence (fruit) to substantiate those claims?

Again, Jesus said, "Thus, you will recognize them by their fruits" (Matt. 7:20). But, he continues in his great "Sermon on the Mount" by saying in verses 21-23:

> *Not everyone who says to me, "Lord, Lord," will enter the kingdom of heaven, but the one who does the will of my Father who is in heaven. On that day many will say to me, "Lord, Lord, did we not prophesy in your name, and cast out demons in your name, and do many mighty works in your name?" And then will I declare to them, "I never knew you; depart from me, you workers of lawlessness."*

These are some of the most frightening and sobering words in all of Scripture. On the day that many stand before Jesus at the Great White Throne Judgment (see Rev. 20:11-15) many will think they are believers and give reasons why they believe they are Christians. However, Jesus will cast them from his presence. Why? They were never truly, born again, regenerated believers in Jesus Christ. Does this scare me? Yes. Does it scare you? It should. It's sobering indeed. The scene Jesus describes in Matthew's gospel doesn't scare me for myself, but for those who base their Christianity on the fact they have walked an aisle, or shook the preacher's hand, prayed a 30-word *sinner's prayer*, and were subsequently baptized in a pool, lake, creek, baptistery or pond. None of these things in and of themselves makes a person a believer in Christ. They can be a part of the process or experience, but if there is no evidence of fruit, then salvation has not taken place. For many, they see salvation as something you do when you are a child because everyone else does and you simply check it off your list of things to do and move on with life.

For so many Christians today, their "Christianity" is nothing more than their way of trying to have "Hell insurance." Salvation is like getting a flu shot of Jesus, yet we keep on living the way we want to and are satisfied with doing our own thing afterwards. Please understand, we must carefully examine our lives, and those of our children, and make sure what was done, when we prayed a prayer, is *influencing* and *impacting* our lives today. Just because a person, even your child or mine, *claims* he or she is saved, does not give evidence in that claim alone that true regeneration has actually taken place. It's what you and I *do* that reveals the truth of who we are. Our actions reveal our identity. Many pray a prayer as a child or go through some sort of ritual sanctioned by the church and think their bases are covered because they've been there and done that. Still, there *must* be evidence and fruit to bear witness to the world that we are indeed changed. I'm not talking about a works based salvation. I'm simply stating a biblical fact. If we claim to be a believer in Jesus Christ, then others should be able to tell that we are by our *actions*.

WHERE'S THE FRUIT?

Many years ago, there was a famous hamburger chain that used a wonderful advertising campaign to laud their bigger and better hamburgers. Interestingly they used a small, petite, older lady who shouted, "Where's the beef?" It was a humorous way to point out their competition was light on the beef. I still remember those silly commercials. Indeed, the hamburger chain was seeking to show there was ample evidence their hamburgers were bigger and better. I wonder if the same could be said of many believers today. "Where's the beef?" Can people tell you are a believer?

Let me describe a scenario from the hunting world that illustrates my point. Where I live today, in the foothills of the Blue Ridge Mountains of North Carolina, there are many deer hunters. There is no question, whatsoever, which people are truly avid deer hunter. Everybody knows who they are. Beginning in late summer, you will hear them talking about preparing for deer season. In fact, they talk about it all the time. Once you are around an enthusiastic deer hunter, it won't be long until they ask you, "Do you hunt?" They love it and they are quick to invite you along and get you into hunting as well. But, it's not just talk. They back up their talk with evidence. As deer season begins, you start to see the pictures and hear the stories of their hunts. They post them on social websites and share these photos and their stories with anyone who wants to see and hear about the latest and greatest buck (male deer with antlers). Hunters are glad to show you the fruit of their labors. They give plenty of evidence of their ardent love of deer hunting.

The same could be said of any other activity or hobby one might have that is enjoyed or loved. You may be a basketball fan or a voracious reader. You name it. If one likes the North Carolina Tar Heels for instance, would you expect to see some Carolina Blue around their home, adorning their car or displayed in their wardrobe? If someone is a Beth Moore fan, wouldn't you expect to find some Beth Moore books or studies on their book cases or night stands?

So, what about the fruit of our Christianity? What about the fruit of our children's Christianity? Is there any fruit? Is there any evidence? You say, "Oh yes, I go to church and my children go to church." Just because someone goes to church doesn't mean they are truly a follower of Christ. There is an old saying, "Just because you live in a garage, it doesn't make you a car." Likewise, just because a person goes to church, it doesn't make them a Christian.

Let's look at the evidence. Let's assume your child has made a profession of faith in Christ at some point in their lives or they have been baptized? If I were to ask you, "Do you know where your child is reading in the Bible?" If they are a believer in Christ, they should be reading the Word of God. Isn't this a fruit or evidence of a true Christian? Do they ever talk about the things of God, uninitiated by you? Do they have a desire to go to church or do you have to coax them out the door? Returning to our deer hunter example, do you have to beg a deer hunter to go hunting? Does he dread hunting season? Do you have to make him prepare for the season? Do you have to make him clean his rifle? Of course not! He's excited about hunting. He frequently thinks about hunting. He doesn't even mind preparing to hunt because he knows it will be worth it when he gets "the big one." What is important to you? What is important to your child or young person? Does anyone have to guess if those things matter to you or your child? No, they don't! What about Jesus? Are you a fan of him? How about your child? Is Jesus at the top of their priority list?

Maybe at this point we need to examine our own spiritual walk. Maybe our relationship with the Lord is such that reading the Bible and having a desire for the things of God has waned a bit. It may be hard for us to think about our children or the young people in our lives and their spiritual fervor, or lack thereof, because we feel that would be hypocritical. Believe me, I understand what you are feeling. I seem to live there in that condition far too often myself. But, it is imperative that we understand something at this juncture. It is absolutely critical that we are honest with ourselves about ourselves and our children. We must be honest about the spiritual condition of our lives and theirs. Is it that 70%-92% of our young people have walked away from their faith, or could it be that many of them are not truly believers? Do your children or those young adults in your life honestly give evidence (show fruit) other than simply a "profession of faith," that they are indeed a dedicated follower and disciple of Christ?

This may be the most important section of the book. Perhaps the Holy Spirit is speaking into your life and in your mind as you read. Maybe you need to honestly sit down with your young person or teen and make certain he or she understands what being a believer is all about. If you are someone who works with young people, do you see evidence that those in your circle of influence are truly believers? We've all heard it said, "Talk is cheap." Indeed it is. Again, what we *do* reveals the truth about what we believe.

Perhaps the most important question we can ask is: *What do they really believe?* If a person is saved as an eight-year-old, shouldn't he or she give evidence of that salvation in their teen years? Shouldn't there be tangible fruit? Shouldn't a dedicated and committed deer hunter desire to go hunting? If you are an avid reader, shouldn't you have a couple of large bookshelves in your home and a book or two on the night stand? Shouldn't a banana tree produce bananas? Most definitely! Yes, we know researchers and statisticians have to rely on what they are told when conducting their surveys. They qualify as best they can if a person is a believer or follower of Christ. Nevertheless, I'm convinced we may not be getting accurate information from them, because what may be closer to the truth is the possibility that many of our young people aren't *walking away* from the faith; it's that they've simply never been saved.

SPIRITUAL EXPECTATIONS-DO WE HAVE ANY?

It is perplexing how we can have young adults in our homes and in our churches who grow up hearing the gospel, participate in all the children and youth activities, immersed in our church programs and still grow up to have little or no interest in

Christianity. As I wrestle with this thought, I believe I'm beginning to see why so many young adults may be slipping under the radar. I'm starting to grasp why they grow up in our homes and churches and do all the Christian things, but eventually disappear. I'm convinced one of the main reasons they do so is because of *low expectations*. We just don't expect much spiritually from our young adults. We have no spiritual goals for them. We want them to become Christians and to be moral and honest people, but beyond these elementary goals, what do we expect?

The Apostle John said in 3 John 4: "I have no greater joy than to hear that my children are walking in the truth." What a statement! Think about it honestly for a moment. Read that verse again. Does this statement describe you? If you are a parent, what is your greatest joy concerning your children? What is it that you talk about at work regarding your children? Most of us love to tell others about our children and grandchildren. What do you brag about when you are talking to your friends and family about the children? I have found the things we seem to talk about most regarding our children are: sports, grades, boyfriends/girlfriends, and jobs.

We are so excited to share with everyone we see that Johnny hit two home runs for his baseball team. We share every detail: what kind of pitch he hit, how far the ball went over the fence, where it landed, etc. We love sharing about how Susie won the most trophies at the dance competition this past weekend. We can't wait to tell the grandparents how well Billy is doing in school. He's got straight A's for the third time in a row. He's on the Principal's List again! We shout from the roof tops when they graduate from high school and college! We post on all the social websites all the details for everyone to see! We tell everyone who their newest boyfriend or girlfriend is. We brag on them when they bring home their first paycheck and we love to let the neighbors know when they have finally gotten that corner office with a window, or when they have become a Vice President at the company, or graduated from nursing or law school. Is there anything wrong with this?

The subject of pride comes to mind, but beyond that let's discuss the subject at hand. What are we saying when these are the things we talk about? We are sending a message to others. We are revealing to the world, and hopefully now to ourselves, that temporal and earthly things matter most to us. If we were writing an epistle today, maybe we would do better to say: "I have no greater joy than to hear that my children are: climbing the corporate ladder, or making a ton of money, or playing professional sports, or making front page headlines in the local paper, while dating the best-looking person in school."

It is hard to see these things in ourselves. They are blind spots in our lives. Yet, here's the truth for many of us today. We really don't have as our *greatest* joy that our "children are walking in the truth." Actually it's almost anything and everything but "walking in the truth" that brings us the most joy. Why is it that we don't seem to have spiritual expectations and desires for our children? Why don't we have spiritual goals for them? Could this be part of the reason why they become "Christians" at a young age and yet walk away or give evidence they were never truly believers in the first place? Most work hard to see that their children are "saved" when they are little. Yes, that is a goal we have for them. But, could it be that we are satisfied with them walking an aisle, praying a prayer, signing a card or getting baptized and that's it? Jesus said, "And you will know the truth, and the truth will set you free" (John 8:32). This may be the truth for many in the Christian faith today.

As a father, I see how much time I spend talking about what my children are learning in school and how well they play the piano or violin or hit the ball. Yet, how much time do I spend talking about what they are learning from Scripture? When is the last time you heard a parent say, "My son has memorized an entire chapter of the Bible?" Can you recall hearing a father say, "My daughter just completed her third mission trip and she's only 18?" These are the types of goals we should have as Christian parents and church leaders. Shouldn't our goals be different than unbelievers? Are they?

I can honestly say I was fooled by the Enemy and didn't even recognize it. I wanted my children, and those other young adults I was influencing as a church leader, to "have it better" than I had it. I guess we call that desire the American Dream. But, where is the American Dream in Scripture? Jesus said that we are to "hunger and thirst" for righteousness. Jesus said, "In this world you will have trouble." Jesus said we are to take up our *cross* daily. We can see that being a follower of Jesus Christ is more than just praying a prayer or coming forward at church during an invitation.

Once we see biblical goals in contrast to cultural goals, we will begin to ask ourselves questions about our children and the young people we know. Do our children know the nine aspects of the fruit of the Spirit (see Gal. 5:22-23)? Do they have a good grasp and handle on basic Bible knowledge? Do they know how to lead someone to Christ using Scripture? Do they have a desire for the things of God? Do we have to beg or bribe them to come to church? Do we know if they have an appetite for daily Bible reading? Are they becoming more and more conformed into the image of Christ? Do we expect total perfection? Not in the least! Will they make mistakes? Sure they will! I'm asking you and myself, "Do our children and teens really exhibit characteristics of a believer in Jesus Christ and do we expect them to grow as a disciple of Christ?" Do we really have spiritual versus temporal goals for our children?

Jesus said that we are to seek first the Kingdom of God and his righteousness. Do we really want our children to grow as a disciple of Christ or are we more interested in them being a part of a winning team and making good grades? God help us to really analyze our motivations and our desires for our children. church leaders must do the same. What is it that we truly desire for our young adults? Is it simply big numbers for our programs or disciples for Christ, who remain in their faith, for the long term?

WHAT CAN A TEENAGER DO?

OK, I know what some of you may be thinking. You may say, "Hey, these guys and girls are just kids! Aren't you expecting a little too much?" Others may be thinking, "Come on, what can a 15-year-old boy do?" I would say, "That's precisely my point!" What do we expect of a teenager? Today, we seem to have very low expectations. I recognize I am making blanket statement. But, I do so because it seems our expectations as Christians have become like those of the culture. Ask someone. What do you expect of a teenager? Many say, "Well, mine don't do much except lie around the house, play video games, text, and chat with their friends on their favorite social website." Why is it that these behaviors alone are acceptable? Shouldn't we expect more? Why is it that we excuse teenagers from being expected to do anything hard just because they are a teenager? I hear people say all the time, "Well, she's a teenager, I guess you can't expect too much from her." Where do we see this mindset in Scripture? We don't. It is not there.

You know, it has not always been this way. Let me give you some examples of young people who did hard things. George Washington as a young teenager surveyed thousands of acres in Virginia. John Quincy Adams was an ambassador of our nation to Russia at the age of 14. John Hancock, who was a signer of the Declaration of Independence, graduated from Harvard at the age of 17. Vance Havner, a great American preacher, sent his first sermon to his local newspaper at age 9, was licensed to preach at age 12, ordained at 15, and preached the gospel for 80 years. Those are amazing accomplishments if you ask me. However, our culture no longer expects these kinds of things from teenagers. After all, they are too young, right?

But think with me for a few moments. We expect them to learn algebra and geometry. We expect them to memorize the Periodic Chart of Elements in chemistry. We expect them to be able to label the parts of a frog in biology and diagram a sentence in English class. Once they can do all these things and have made the grade, they graduate. But what about spiritually? Is there a "graduation" of sorts that we should expect spiritually? The answer is, "yes," and it is one of the main reasons I've written this book.

I believe we have become comfortable with our young adults being stuck in a glass box. A box in which they're incarcerated and we don't even realize it. Why? It's invisible, that's why. It's a box called: *low expectations.* A child will rise to our expectations. Whatever the expectations are, whether high or low, they will rise or fall to them. In other words, we will get what we expect. If you go to your kitchen sink and lift the handle or turn the knob, do you expect to get water from that faucet in a matter of a couple of seconds? Of course! If you take the key to your car, insert it into the ignition and turn it, do you expect the car to crank? Certainly! If you order something Next Day Delivery, don't you expect it to show up the next day? Sure you do and so do I. But, let the water stop flowing and the car stop cranking and the packages not be delivered and we're upset. In fact, we may even say, "I'm not going to stand for this!" What about our children? What do we expect from them? What can they do? *They will do exactly what we expect and train them to do.* If we expect little, we will receive little. If we expect more, we will get more. The idea of low expectations for our young people seems to be just the way it is in America. But this is not the case in many other places around the world.

I have traveled to Ethiopia and assisted my brothers and sisters in Christ in their churches as they work in their communities to spread the gospel. As I've done so, I've noticed something that would seem almost astounding to an American or anyone who was raised in our western culture. Children as young as four- or five-years-old take care of their siblings. It's truly amazing! The girls, particularly, carry their younger sibling on their back in a type of papoose or carrier. Their siblings may be only two- or three-years-old. Not only that, I saw children as young as six- or seven-years-old that were shepherds and who tended to flocks of sheep, goats or cattle all day in the fields. In Ethiopia, these small children lead or drive the animals with a stick or staff and carry a small sack or pouch with some food in it and stay out in the fields or pastures all day long. You see them on the small roads or paths coming back home at dusk after being out in the fields all day!

The children I've described don't get into trouble, nor do they run away to play. They are given responsibility and they rise to those expectations. It's as simple as that. From the time these children are born, they are *trained* and then *expected* to do what they are told. It's been said that if you pour water into a harbor, it will raise the level of all the boats. I believe this is what we must do with our children, even at young ages. We must pour the water of great expectations into the harbor and then be prepared to teach, equip and train them to reach and attain those high expectations. This requires much time, discipline, patience and hard work. It kind of reminds me of the fruit of the Spirit: love, joy, peace, patience, kindness, goodness, faithfulness, gentleness and self-control. If we are going to embark upon this great journey of raising expectations, it will certainly require all of the fruit of the Spirit to be found in us in good measure to see that our children flourish in the Lord.

My two oldest daughters (both are teenagers) play various instruments like the piano, violin, guitar, mandolin and viola. It's truly wonderful to hear them play these beautiful instruments in our home, church and community. But, their ability to play and to play well doesn't just happen. They have teachers that train and equip them each week and then they have a practice regimen that we *expect* them to maintain. Why do we expect them to practice? There are many reasons, but truthfully speaking, one of the main ones is because we are paying good money for those lessons! Isn't that almost sad to say? Our expectations in this case are tied to the fact that we are paying for their skill development. It seems we expect more when there is an investment. But, can the same be said spiritually? Are we making an investment spiritually? Am I paying a price for my children's spiritual development? Maybe we are (and to some degree we all are making an investment spiritually) but will it be enough? I will discuss this price in great detail in chapter 4. But, at this point, I simply want us to know that there is a price that will have to be paid, if we expect our children and teenagers to have a solid spiritual foundation and be more than just a "kidult" in their 20's and beyond.

JESUS OUR EXAMPLE AND MODEL

We can ask, "Are there Scriptural models we can follow?" The answer is a resounding "Yes!" In fact, as great as Washington, Adams, Hancock and Havner are, I'm most interested in what the Scriptures teach on the subject. What do we find young people doing in the Bible? Let's examine a few examples.

Let's begin with the greatest example, Jesus Christ. Do you remember what happened to Jesus when he was just twelve years old? The account of Joseph and Mary losing Jesus is found in Luke 2:41-52. If you are familiar with the Bible you may remember this account. Joseph and Mary had been to Jerusalem for the feast of the Passover. In those days, they traveled as families on the long journey from Nazareth to Jerusalem. It was customary for a child or young person to spend some of this journey traveling with cousins or other family members. Although we don't know for sure and aren't told, this certainly may have been the case with Jesus.

After a day's journey from Jerusalem back home, Joseph and Mary could not locate Jesus. I can imagine them asking around among the other families, "Is Jesus with you?" After concluding that Jesus was not in the entourage, Joseph and Mary returned to Jerusalem. Some scholars say Joseph and Mary were separated from their son for three days, while others say the separation could have been as long as five days. The point is that they were separated for several days. What would you be thinking if you had a 12-year old son that was lost in a big city like Jerusalem? We would have probably already had an Amber Alert and an All Points Bulletin circulating through the local police departments. There would have been search teams, search dogs, helicopters and drag teams for the local ponds and lakes.

Where did they find Jesus? They found him "in the temple sitting among the teachers, listening to them and asking them questions," so says Doctor Luke (Luke 2:46). Are you kidding? He was in the temple? Yes! They found their 12-year-old in "church" listening and asking questions. Now let's think about this for a moment. Is that what you would expect of most 12-year-olds today?

Let's imagine a 12-year-old boy was lost in a large city in America. I'll use Charlotte, North Carolina for example. Imagine a 12-year-old boy being lost for days in a city like Charlotte. Where would we expect to find him? Rack your brain please and after you have completed the mental gyrations of the potential places you would expect to find a typical 12-year-old boy in a large, American city today, try to imagine going to the local church and finding him there. It seems odd doesn't it? But, why should it? Is it so strange to think that a 12-year-old boy would be in church talking to the teachers, listening to their teaching and asking questions? Truthfully, it does seem strange, because we don't expect our young people to have a desire to be in church or a desire for the things of God. Did you notice the word "expect" was italicized in the sentence you just completed reading? Expect? Expect what? What do we expect? Is it the worst? Why is it that we most likely expect something different than the behavior of Jesus for our children? Why don't we expect the best?

Nonetheless, even Joseph and Mary were astonished. I can imagine seeing them walking into the temple courts asking everyone they saw, "Have you seen a 12-year-old boy that is about this tall?" Finally, either someone points them to Jesus or they see him. There he is. He's sitting among the teachers. But, he is not just sitting there. Oh no. He is listening and asking questions and everyone who heard him was amazed at his understanding and his answers. To put it in every day words, Jesus was blowing their minds! When they finally found him after at least three days missing, Mary was perplexed and wanted to know why Jesus had treated them like that. She said, "Son, why have you treated us so?

Behold, your father and I have been searching for you in great distress" (Luke 2:48). Mary and Joseph were upset and worried. You might say, "I'd be more than upset, I'd be livid!"

Of course we know Jesus never sinned, but some could possibly ask, "Who does he think he is?" He has worried his parents to death. He's been missing for days and they've had to waste time and trouble looking for him. Can you imagine what they were thinking as they bedded down each night? They were apart from their son and desperately wondering where to look for him in that mammoth city? Can you contemplate in your mind how distressed they must have been? If you have ever lost a child for any period of time, which I have, then you know a little of what they were feeling. It must have been agonizing!

What does Jesus say to them? It's almost humorous. Jesus asked, "Why were you looking for me?" Jesus was perplexed, just as his parents were. You can see this in his question. Jesus asked, "Did you not know that I must be in my Father's house" (Luke 2:49)? Jesus was saying in affect, "Why were you distressed and looking for me? I'm astounded that you searched for as long as you did. You have raised me to have a desire and an appetite for the things of God, my Father; and so, where else would you expect to find me?" I believe Jesus was acknowledging the wonderful job they had done in teaching and training him. Jesus, after all, had been circumcised on the eighth day, as all Jewish boys were according to their custom (Luke 2:21). He was presented in the temple in Jerusalem and sacrifices were made on his behalf, as he was consecrated to the Lord (Luke 2:22-24). Joseph and Mary had done the work of teaching and training him to be about the Father's business. Jesus seemed amazed they would look anywhere else except the temple.

It is difficult to wrap our minds around this. Jesus was 12-years-old and he already had a desire to be around the people of God and was equipped to carry on a conversation with adults about spiritual matters. Now if Jesus is to be our model and our example in all things, wouldn't this be the case for all of our 12-year-olds?

We should teach, train and equip our children from the time they are born to be prepared, ready and able to proclaim what Jesus did. We must train them to be "doing the business of God." In fact, we should be raising our children to be "about the Father's business" from the time they're born. Does that seem too early? It's never too early. You see, that's the problem with so many of us. We wait too long. We don't start early enough. We wait until it's too late and the cement has hardened.

Now I know what some of you are thinking. "Well, this was Jesus and no one is perfect like Jesus." Am I right? After all, this is the Son of God we are talking about. Of course Jesus is going to be living right, because he's perfect, because he's God's son. At first glance, this seems to be all there is to it and we should move on. Since Jesus was perfect, then truthfully speaking, he is probably not the best example. He is an anomaly. However, theologically, I don't think we can make that argument on solid ground. Why? Because, I believe Jesus had the choice to make on his own. He chose to be in the flesh. He was tempted and tried as we all were. He had the ability to choose (see Heb. 4:15). He could have chosen to sin, if he had wanted. He could have walked away from the cross when he prayed: "Let this cup pass from me." He could have called 10,000 angels to come to his rescue while he was stapled to a Roman cross. But he didn't! He chose not to. Jesus was indeed the God-man who *chose* to be perfect. Jesus had been trained to behave and act like a young adult and that is exactly what he did. Therefore, he is indeed our model to follow.

What do we see in the life of Jesus at age 12? Take a look:

√ He had a mature sense of responsibility, purpose and destiny
√ He had the trust of his parents to be with others
√ He knew what to do and what not to do without being told
√ He had a desire for the things of God
√ He exhibited a keen sense of discernment in relation to the company he kept

√   He had a desire to understand truth and wisdom

√   He was articulate enough to speak to other adults and carry on a conversation with them to the point of their amazement

√   He was submissively obedient to his parents-no bad attitudes, rebellion or disobedience

Jesus had the unmistakable evidence of godliness in his life. I would submit, if a young person, who claims Christ as Lord, doesn't exhibit these characteristics by age 12, they probably aren't going to at age 16 or 20. Maturity often comes with age, but I know some godly 16-year-olds that act more mature than some 30-year-olds. If a person claims Jesus as their Lord and Savior, then there should be a desire for pursuing the things of God.

Luke concludes the account with these words in Luke 2:51-52:

And he went down with them and came to Nazareth and was submissive to them. And his mother treasured up all these things in her heart. And Jesus increased in wisdom and in stature and in favor with God and man.

These two verses are crucial in our understanding of the difference between a child and an adult. Remember, we find no Scripture about adolescence. This term and this period, condition, or season of life is a modern-day invention of man. Again, this season called adolescence does not exist in Scripture and what we see played out vividly in this passage confirms that for us. Luke tells us after Jesus was presented in the temple, Joseph and Mary returned to Nazareth "and the *child* grew and became strong, filled with wisdom" (Luke 2:40). See the word "child" in that verse? Jesus was considered a child prior to his bar mitzvah, which would occur by the age of thirteen for a Jewish young man. Still, Jesus at the age of twelve was already acting like an adult. He showed the onset of moral reasoning and personal responsibility. But, what we really must not miss is found in Luke 2:50: "And he went down with them and came to Nazareth and was *submissive* to them."

He was *submissive* to them. It meant Jesus had free will. He could make intelligent, moral choices. The relationship between Jesus and his parents had gone from one of compulsory obedience to submission. Jesus, even though he was a young adult capable of making his own decisions, chose to submit to their authority. He submitted himself to them. This is the behavior of an adult, not a child. Adults live "submitting to one another out of reverence for Christ" (Eph. 5:21). This is the goal. We must teach and to train so that we raise young adults who are willing to place themselves under submission to authority. The point Luke is making is an emphasis on the *continual action* of Jesus' submission to his parents. In other words, he was continually submitting at all times as an act of his will, of his own choosing. He was "continually submitting himself" to them even though they are equals. That's right. They were equals. When a young person becomes a young adult, he or she becomes a spiritual equal to his or her parents. This doesn't mean they get to call their own shots, because if they are acting like a young adult, they won't see the concept of equals as one to take advantage of but rather one in which to mature.

I am reminded again of Paul's instruction to young Timothy in 1 Timothy 4:12:

> *Let no one despise you for your youth, but set the believers an example in speech, in conduct, in love, in faith, in purity.*

Paul admonished Timothy, who was, according to some scholars, a teenager, to set an example for the other believers. Timothy was to "set an example" in the way he talked, acted and lived out a faithful, pure life before believers that were older than himself. This idea of *submission as equals* can revolutionize a relationship with a young person. I can see the young person, perhaps your own child, swallowing hard when you show him or her this account in Scripture and the fact that Jesus, of his own free will, even as an equal, was willing to submit to his parents. That gives me goose bumps! There is great power in these verses if we can grasp it and use it.

Therefore, Jesus went down to Nazareth and was submissively obedient to them. He chose to be obedient to the training and teaching he was receiving and would receive. What else do we know about Jesus' life from this scene as a 12-year-old in the temple until he was 30-years-old and began his ministry? We know absolutely nothing except that he "increased in wisdom and in stature and in favor with God and man." That's a very "weighty" statement. He "grew." Even from the time he was 12-years-old, conversing articulately with the teachers in the temple, Jesus continued to grow in wisdom. He continued to grow, because there was an expectation in the Hebrew culture to do so. The young boys and girls were expected to mature and grow spiritually. What about our culture? Is there this expectation? What about in the church? Is there this kind of expectation in your church? Let's think about our own homes. What do we expect from our children? If you're like me, you are probably not expecting enough.

OTHER SCRIPTURAL MODELS

Are there other Scriptural models? Yes, there are many.

- √ Samuel was a young boy when he answered God's call in his life
- √ Josiah became king at age 8. At age 18 he had the Law read to the people and made a covenant with the Lord to obey him with all his heart and soul
- √ Daniel, Shadrach, Meshach and Abednego were young men who were most likely teenagers when taken into exile in Babylon. These four refused to bow to the pagan king, Nebuchadnezzar
- √ David was a teenager when he fought bears and lions and killed Goliath when no grown man would fight him
- √ David's army was compiled of mostly teenagers

√ Mary, whom many scholars believe she was a teen, was a young lady when she was entrusted with giving birth to and helping raise the Son of God

√ Timothy was a young protégé of Paul, whom many scholars say was a young man in his late-teens when Paul began mentoring him

√ The Apostles were 12 young men who were hand-picked by Jesus to follow him as their Rabbi or Teacher. From scholarly biblical evidence, it seems most were teenagers when Jesus invited them to "come follow me"

To give Scriptural credence to the last point, we will look at a passage found in Matthew 17:24-27. After Jesus and his disciples arrived in Capernaum, the collectors of the two-drachma temple tax came to Peter and asked, "Does your teacher not pay the tax?" Peter told them "Yes." When Peter came into the house, Jesus asked Peter what he thought about the situation. After a brief discussion, Jesus told Peter he didn't want to offend. Therefore, Jesus instructed Peter to go down to the sea and cast a hook and take the first fish that he caught and pay the temple tax for himself and Peter.

There is much that can be discussed from this passage and I would encourage deeper study, but let's summarize. First of all we need to know why Jesus was in Capernaum. Jesus had made his home-base in Capernaum because he could not minister in his hometown of Nazareth. Those in Nazareth and even those in his own family thought Jesus was crazy. In Capernaum Jesus lived in the home of Peter's mother-in-law. When Jesus was in town, he and the apostles often stayed there. Remember Jesus was frequently called "Rabbi" or "Teacher" by the apostles. They had "left all" to follow Jesus. These men, after a night of prayer by Jesus, had been hand-picked by him to be his followers or disciples. Some were fishermen, one was a tax collector, and even one was a Zealot. This was an eclectic group of guys, but they seemed to be similar in one area. That similarity seems to be their ages.

As I've studied the lives of these men, there is a lot of evidence that seems to point to a certain hypothesis about their ages. Could it be that some of these men were actually teenagers? Is this possible? Certainly, most often we see these men, depicted in paintings as older men with beards and even bald heads. There are specific clues in this passage that may indicate otherwise. On the occasion, referring to the Scripture above, the tax collectors from the temple came asking if Jesus, their teacher, was going to pay the temple tax. As we study we will find the temple tax was to be paid by all those who were 20 years of age or older in accordance with the Old Testament law (see Ex. 30:11-16). As we read, Jesus told Peter to go and catch a fish and open its mouth and pay the temple tax with a four-drachma coin. This amount was enough to pay for two men. Peter was to pay Jesus' tax and his. What about the others? Remember, only those 20 years of age and older had to pay the tax. Could it be the other men were teenagers? Again, this is certainly a valid hypothesis and one that many scholars believe and espouse.

Think about this. In the first century most men didn't live past their mid-40's, so 20 years of age would be considered "middle" age. Some have said Matthew had to be older than twenty to have been a tax collector, yet we don't know this as a fact. I'm not trying to be dogmatic about this, yet I believe a good case could be made that the gospel of Jesus Christ was indeed carried by teenagers throughout the first century world. That is a fantastic thought! Look at what teenagers can do! Jesus entrusted his gospel with a group of young men that were likely teenagers! What can teenagers do? They *will do* exactly what we expect them to do.

So, how do we get our young people, our children, to the point that they are Christ-centered and committed followers? We begin when they are young. This is a lifelong training process that culminates with a rite of passage, which is a process similar to the Hebrew custom that was used with Jesus. Am I talking about having a bar mitzvah? No, not necessarily, but ROP does have some similarities to the Jewish ritual. The kind of "rite of passage" I'm talking about and will describe in this book is a culture of expectations in our homes and churches that is simply a way of raising the bar for our young people. Do we need such a way? Do we need a lifelong conduit whereby we can raise the level of expectations for our children and young adults? Yes, we do. I believe it is called **Rite of Passage**.

3

The Role of the Church

ANOTHER PROGRAM?

Not another program! Please don't tell me **Rite of Passage** is just another program! Perhaps that's what you think at this point. I understand most churches have many, many programs. We have them for all age groups and all stations of life. So, I am the first to agree that we do not need another program to add to our list. Programs, organizations, committees and other church structures have their place and can be useful and beneficial in the church. Yet, they can also create so many layers of bureaucracy that we struggle to be effective and truly minister.

I am not an expert, nor do I claim to be an authority on the pros and cons of church programs, but I have more than three decades of practical experience and I hope I've learned some things along the way. Before becoming a pastor, I was a layman in the church for many years. I've worked and served in just about every capacity one can imagine. I have served on nearly every committee and have been chairman of most at least once. If it can be done in a local church, I guess I've done it. But, that is not the issue. I tell you all this to describe my experience and background so you will know that I write from a perspective of practical experience. These ideas are not philosophical theories from a textbook written by someone that is out of touch. The issue at hand has to do with raising Christ-centered young adults and how to go about doing so in churches already wrought with many programs. We don't need another program to administrate and oversee. We have enough to do already.

ROP is more like a way of thinking about, and a process of training, our young adults. It is more of a lifestyle choice of raised expectations, principally within a home, as well as the church. In other words, practically speaking, ROP can be described as a race that begins at birth and culminates at the finish line of young adulthood.

Let us think about how the church ministers to the young adult today. We have created a youth subculture in most of our American churches. We have programs for the children that literally begin out of the womb. The children are placed in infant rooms or nurseries from birth and later graduate to Children's Church and snacks during the worship time. From there they move to middle school groups and then to the youth group. The youth group will hold them through their teen years with a plethora of outings, camps, trips, devotions, pizza blasts, concerts and other fun "youth" events, until we finally graduate them to a college or singles class. What I have just described in four sentences encompasses millions and millions of dollars invested in supporting and sustaining these programs through staffing and allocated budget dollars. Let us examine the results. Are we graduating Christ-centered young adults? What is the return on investment of all our staff and money spent? Even though it is difficult to admit, some words that come to my mind are: dismal, poor, weak and unfruitful. While these words might adequately describe the results, I believe there is another word that might best describe the last 40 years of youth ministry:

FAILURE

I know that last statement is blunt, but I don't believe in beating around the bush. It took a burning bush to get Moses' attention on the backside of a desert after 40 years and I believe it's time for our own wake-up call with our own "burning bush" experience.

We must begin to see the light before we lose more kids! The truth is, youth culture, and all that goes with it, is simply not producing teens that are committed and dedicated to Jesus Christ. So ROP must be the answer, right? We will just have them go through an 8-week program and that will do it. No, unfortunately, in and of itself ROP will not produce any better results than what we've been getting. What have we been getting? We have been sending our kids to church and youth experiences such as intense summer camps and we watch them come home "fired up" only to be back to normal within a few weeks. Why? Because we've simply plugged them back into the dead homes from which they came. I don't care how good a drop cord is, if we plug it in to a dead outlet then we are wasting our time.

Perhaps it is time for a paradigm shift in our churches. But this shift in thinking will be difficult to make because we love our edifices to ourselves and we love telling everyone how good our programs are. We boast about the numbers. We talk mainly about the ABC's: attendance, buildings and cash. We want to know how many attend, when will we have to build again, and how much money we have taken in, spent, and have left in the budget. Some might say that if we have a lot of people coming to something then it must be good. *What about the changed lives?* Shouldn't that be the barometer?

I was in a church a few years ago that was mammoth. It was and still is one of the largest churches in the country. They had a service for the adults in one place on the campus, a service for the youth in another place and a place for the children in yet another place. I had a lot of young adults with me, so we were "encouraged" to go to the youth service. The youth, interestingly, had a building of their own complete with their own kitchen, auditorium, stage, praise band, etc. It was very impressive to say the least. As the program for the evening began, the youth pastor came forward and told a few cute one-liners, then he started calling out numbers. It seemed that each week, every young person received a raffle ticket for coming and could win a door prize. They were giving away really nice things. The night I was there they were giving away iPods! As you can imagine, the kids were very excited and were clamoring to grab their tickets to see if they were a winner. As I stood there, I thought, "Is this what we have become? Do we have to give away electronic devices just to draw a crowd and build up our numbers?" The numbers were good! I estimated around 250 teenagers were in attendance, but is it really about the numbers?

After the service I had the opportunity to locate the youth pastor. He was in his mid-20s, attractive, single and really looked the part. He was dressed like the teens and even had the hip hairstyle and necklace to boot. I think you get the picture. I don't say all of this to be critical. I just want you to have a mental image here.

As I began to speak with this young man, who was very nice and personable, he shared about the immense pressure he was under. He said, "They are on me all the time." He said, "I've got to keep 250 in here or they don't think I'm doing my job." I asked him why he was giving away door prizes. He said, "That's what brings them in!" I said, "So, is it working?" He said, "Uh, well, I guess."

This young man had wonderful motives and was very kind and amiable. We were standing off to the side of the stage just chatting and I shared with him that I was working with youth at this time in my life and I had been struggling in this area as well. I told him he wasn't alone. I said, "We all feel we have to produce some big numbers and perform so that we can justify our existence as 'youth' guys." He said, "Right! That's exactly how I feel." I asked again, "So, is it working?" He said, "Is what working?" I said, "Is your program working?" He paused this time. I could see the wheels turning in his mind. He muttered to himself, "Is it working?" Then, tears filled his eyes and he looked at me with such a painful expression on his face that I struggle to find the words to try to describe what he said to me. He said, "Man, I really don't think it's working at all." He continued, "I've been doing this for two and a half years and nothing is changing." He said, "They come and go like a revolving door. They come for the fun stuff and then only a few ever show up when we go serve food at the local food kitchen or take hats and gloves to the homeless downtown. I'm just spinning my wheels."

I could not have said it any better myself, "Just spinning our wheels." That's a good way to describe what most of us are doing in our churches when it comes to our ministries and programs concerning young adults. What the young man was experiencing in his church was what I was experiencing, just on a smaller scale. As we concluded our conversation, he said to me, "You know, I only have about a handful or two of kids who really 'get it.'" He concluded, "Most of these kids …" as he pointed his finger toward the crowd of kids, as they were getting their pizza and soft drinks "… really aren't here for spiritual reasons at all. They are here because of the prizes, food and to see their friends," he said.

Recently, I heard of a "youth event" that was to be held in a gym where the activities included: kickball, basketball, dodge ball and pizza on a Saturday night. I was told the purpose of the event was "spiritual growth." I inquired about the "spiritual content" of the evening and was told, "We are going to take about 10-15 minutes between the fun and games and give them Jesus." I was informed, "We won't be too much 'in your face.' We really just want to get them off the streets and give them a good time." I was assured, "Don't worry. We'll keep them on 'lock-down' so no one gets in trouble or gets away." This is a fairly common occurrence. I, myself, have been involved with these events for years. Yet, at the end of the day, we are left where we started. We have young adults who have been entertained, fed and occupied, but little beyond that has been accomplished that could be considered "spiritual."

What is wrong with this picture? Does it sound like what is happening in your church? After all, we are keeping them off the streets and giving them something to do. That's got to count for something. Well, maybe it does. But, is that our goal? Is that what we desire for our children and young adults? I could tell that my fellow youth worker in that mega-church hadn't consciously thought about it much. But, deep down, he knew he was nothing more than a glorified activities coordinator. He was much like one of those people on a cruise line who coordinates the bingo, shows and meals for the passengers. Surely the goal is not just to *entertain* our young people. Surely there is more to this thing than just drawing a crowd and keeping them busy. What happens after they come back from these youth events? They may indeed be "fired up," but then what? What I have found is within about six to eight weeks of a summer camp, concert or event, they are right back where they started. It wears off. We host these events or take our young people to them, but they are typically only flashes in the pan, because no real discipleship is taking place. The young people are typically going right back into homes that are spiritually weak or even dead. What should we do?

More Staff and Money?

For years our churches have been hiring more staff and spending more money on all sorts of children and youth programs. We've gone from churches in the 1950's and '60's that had a single pastor to churches that now have very large staffs. I was recently handed a page that listed the staff of a church in Florida which had twenty staff members. In this particular church they have a staff member who serves: children, middle school students, high school students, college students and singles. These five staffers report to a Minister of Education. Maybe hiring more staff is the answer. After all, we need to get someone who can relate to our young people. We will just spend more money and bring in more people. That has to be the answer. Unfortunately, it is *not* the answer. You would think we would have learned this from the public sector. All we need to do is look at the staggering amount of money that is spent per student on education in this country and we see that a lot of money spent on a problem does not necessarily solve it. We spend a great deal more money educating our kids today than we did in 1960, yet are we smarter or better off? Are we seeing better educated kids because we are spending more money? As I stated, more money thrown at a problem does not equate to solving that problem or even bringing about more favorable results. It just means, in most cases, that we are simply *spending more money.*

The Bible teaches the Apostle Paul went throughout Asia Minor appointing elders at those churches. He commissioned Titus to do the same on the Isle of Crete and he gave specific instructions to both Timothy and Titus about the qualifications for those elders (see 1 Tim. 3 and Titus 1). The multiple layers we have created in staffing were not evident in the early church. Some might argue that most churches today are much bigger in size and need more people. I would respectfully disagree. Peter preached in Acts 2 and 3,000 came to Christ in one day (see Acts 2:41). Yet, the church in Jerusalem didn't load up on staff. It seems we have created layer upon layer of staffers to do the work that the body has become unwilling or worse, no longer has the desire to do. The job of elders is to focus the church on works of service. Our job is to equip the saints to do the work, not to be paid to do it for them.

My desire in sharing about the structure, make-up, leadership, focus and overall purpose of the early church is not to teach a lesson on ecclesiology, the study of the church and its functions, but to point out what our mission is to *be* about. Jesus said, I came "to seek and save the lost" (John 19:10). Jesus cared about people. Shouldn't we do the same? Maybe we have become satisfied with taking care of our own within the walls of our buildings. Could it be that we have set up our church structures and budgets to entertain ourselves, instead of taking up the responsibilities we are currently paying staffers to do?

We must genuinely take a hard look at what we are doing. Are we really making disciples in our churches? Maybe we are in spots or small pockets. But, do we really desire to teach, train and equip our young people to carry out the Great Commission? Or are we just cycling them through our programs like widgets in a factory with little focus or direction beyond the next *fun* activity? How much money is being spent each year on activities for the children and young adults in our churches? What is the purpose of those activities? What is the return on that investment?

In reality we are getting very little return on the investment we've made over the last 30-plus years and the bottom line is that we are producing very few grounded, Christ-centered young adults. I understand young people come to Christ every year in our youth programs and at camps and special youth events. But, as a whole, the youth industry and our youth programs are not getting the job done. No one would go to the store and continue buying a product that had a 70-92% failure rate. The reason we are seeing such a low number of young adults in their 20's following Christ is because of how we have chosen to evangelize them. It is very common to have people bow their heads, close their eyes and repeat a 30-word prayer at youth events like I described earlier. Perhaps we do this for the sake of time and numbers. At some events, we may even have people come forward and sign a card, or speak with a counselor. Does this really mean they are changed, regenerated, new creations? Maybe they are and maybe they aren't. I hope they are. Only time will tell.

Did Jesus say, "Go and make *converts* of all nations?" No. He said, "Go and make *disciples*." There is a huge difference. Jesus also said that he came to seek and save the lost. There is not a contradiction here. We are to seek the lost and then lead them to Christ, but often, that is where we stop. We get them "saved" or perhaps baptized, in the Baptist church, and that's it. All too often, we are not making *disciples*. We have left out the second part of the formula taught by Jesus Christ. Lead them to Jesus we must. But, we must also teach them to be committed, dedicated followers of Christ. We must do both.

Think about the life of Jesus. He poured himself into 12 men for approximately three years. He did this night and day. He and his followers traveled together, slept alongside one another, ate meals together and literally lived life side by side. Remember what those who followed Jesus were called? Those who followed Jesus were called "disciples." A disciple, by definition, is a follower or someone who accepts or assists in spreading the teaching of someone. A disciple is taught. A disciple is not someone who has a one time experience and then walks away and goes back to doing what he had been doing prior to his conversion experience. A disciple is trained, equipped and admonished by the teacher. This is exactly what we are to be doing in the church. We should disciple our young people. We need to be focusing much less on "fun" activities and much more on discipleship. But there is more.

We must carefully consider what the Bible says when it comes to how we view the training and equipping of our young adults. As we do so we will quickly arrive at another potential paradigm shift for some. *The church is not responsible for the spiritual discipleship of the young adults or children who attend that church.* When you read that statement, you might think, "Yes, I agree with that." However, many churches don't act like it. Instead, they have taken the role and responsibility in child-rearing that is not supported biblically.

WHO'S RESPONSIBLE?

According to Scripture, the church has never been given the responsibility of developing or discipling Christ-centered young adults. That is a bold statement. We have assigned the church to do a job that was never intended for the church. I'm 100% convinced our churches must move away from the church-centered ministry to young people to a home-centered ministry to the *families,* principally the fathers. Why? The job of raising spiritually grounded children has been assigned to *fathers* not to churches. Fathers are instructed in Scripture over and over again to bring their children up in the "discipline and instruction of the Lord." A key verse on this subject is found in the context of Ephesians 6:1-4:

> *Children, obey your parents in the Lord, for this is right. "Honor your father and mother" (this is the first commandment with a*

*promise), "that it may go well with you and that you may live long
in the land." Fathers, do not provoke your children to anger, but
bring them up in the discipline and instruction of the Lord.*

Paul gives instruction to fathers in this passage. Children are
commanded to obey their parents and to honor them, while the
fathers are told to discipline and instruct the children. This concept
and Scriptural principle will be developed in greater detail later.
Yet, we must understand now that this premise is a key to
understanding ROP. Before we can understand the role of the
church regarding our young people, we must correctly understand
what the Bible teaches concerning the family, particularly the father,
in bringing up children. I point this out because the church in many
cases is unknowingly hindering the fathers from doing what they've
been assigned to do. The fathers must lead along with mothers. We
must understand that *parents* are the primary Christian educators
of our young people. The family is the God-ordained institution,
which has existed longer than the church, for training, instructing
and for passing along the Christian faith to the next generation.
What is our goal? Again, John tells us in 3 John 4.

*I have no greater joy than to hear that my children are walking in
the truth.*

If this is truly our target, then it is critical that we are very clear
in our minds what it will take to be able to make such a statement.
Of course we know "walking in the truth" means living the
Christian life daily. Again, the primary responsibility for leading
children in the truth has been given to the fathers. This may not
be a politically correct statement, but the Scriptures teach this fact
repeatedly.

Let us begin to see this truth by starting in the place of
beginnings, in the book of Genesis. When God created Adam and
Eve, he told them to be "fruitful and multiply." They did and
children were born and the human race began to grow larger and
multiply. We are well aware of this fact, but there is more to what
the Lord was saying than just "have babies." The prophet Malachi

tells us in Malachi 2:15: "Did he not make them one, with a portion of the Spirit in their union? And what was the one thing God was seeking? Godly offspring." There we see it. One of the greatest purposes for marriage is the fact God is seeking godly offspring.

The Bible is clear, when we have children; the goal must be to produce godly offspring, not just offspring. Unfortunately, for many, we have made bringing up our children about getting them a good education so they can get a good job, make good money, and then live happily ever after. The problem with this thinking is that it's not Scriptural. I believe the Lord cares very little, if at all, about our diplomas, 401-k and retirement accounts. In fact, I don't think he has a room in heaven where he'll hang our diplomas and stock certificates for all to see throughout eternity. God cares most about those who choose to follow him. his desire for us, as parents, is that we produce godly offspring. It's absolutely essential that we understand this mandate and heed it.

It is clear that the center-piece of God's redemptive plan is through the family. From the creation of Adam, through the call of Abraham, through the establishment of the Davidic Covenant, through the lineage of David's descendents, eventually bringing us the Christ, God has chosen to work in and through families. Many families today, principally because of spiritually inept fathers, no longer have a multi-generational vision to train their children in the ways of the Lord. Quite simply, we are not producing godly offspring because we have forgotten and are not heeding the commands of God.

Moses records more insight on the matter in Genesis 18:17-19:

> *The LORD said, "Shall I hide from Abraham what I am about to do, seeing that Abraham shall surely become a great and mighty nation, and all the nations of the earth shall be blessed in him? For I have chosen him, that he may command his children and his household after him to keep the way of the LORD by doing righteousness and justice, so that the LORD may bring to Abraham what he has promised him.*

The Lord said "I have chosen him, that he may command his *children* and his *household* after him to keep the way of the Lord..." Moses, himself, in Deuteronomy 6:4-7 gives instructions and admonitions from the Lord to the fathers regarding his command for them in teaching and training the children.

> *Hear, O Israel: The LORD our God, the LORD is one. You shall love the LORD your God with all your heart and with all your soul and with all your might. And these words that I command you today shall be on your heart. You shall teach them diligently to your children, and shall talk of them when you sit in your house, and when you walk by the way, and when you lie down, and when you rise.*

In this passage Moses is specifically charging fathers with the responsibility to train their sons to obey the laws of God. I am not in any way minimizing the importance of mothers in teaching their sons or of parents teaching daughters. However, the Hebrew text of Deuteronomy 6 puts an emphasis on sons, and the patriarchal structure of the whole book places an emphasis on fathers. The emphasis on sons is for the purpose of raising up future, godly fathers who will, themselves, continue to teach this covenant to their families for the entire history of Israel.

It is God's pattern, established from creation, to lead families through the husband/father. He established this order by first creating Adam alone, with no wife, and giving him the original prohibition concerning the tree of the knowledge of good and evil (see Gen. 2:16-17). This patriarchal pattern is easy to see throughout the Old Testament. The words of God are given first to Moses, then to men as leaders, then through them to all the people of Israel. The word of the Lord permeated the nation of Israel family by family through the leaders, the fathers, of those families. This is God's design. Some might consider this to be chauvinistic. Yet, God designed the man to bear up under the weight of being the protector, provider and spiritual leader of the home (see Eph. 5:22-33). The wife was created to be the helper, not the leader. Genesis 2:18 indicates: "Then the LORD God said,

"It is not good that the man should be alone; I will make him a helper fit for him." In many homes today we have reversed these God-given roles. Therefore, many of our homes are not structured in a biblical manner.

The last words spoken in the Old Testament were by the prophet Malachi as he instructed the people not to forget the Law of Moses. He implored them in the last verse of the Old Testament: "And he will turn the hearts of fathers to their children and the hearts of children to their fathers, lest I come and strike the land with a decree of utter destruction" (Mal. 4:6). Those last words, "turn the hearts of fathers to their children," are very poignant to me as a father of four children. I often ask myself, "Is my heart turned to my children?" Do I really desire and have as my greatest joy to hear that "my children are walking in the truth?" Now if this last statement of the Old Testament is not strong enough in pointing the fathers back to the children, read the words found at the beginning of the New Testament in Luke 1:16-17:

And he will turn many of the children of Israel to the Lord their God, and he will go before him in the spirit and power of Elijah, to turn the hearts of the fathers to the children, and the disobedient to the wisdom of the just, to make ready for the Lord a people prepared.

There they are again. The words: "turn the hearts of the fathers to the children." The last words spoken in the Old Testament are some of the first words spoken in the New Testament. Perhaps this is just coincidental? No, nothing is *coincidental* in God's Holy Scripture. The fathers are admonished and implored to turn their hearts toward their children. We will address specifically how this is to be done in chapter 4 when we look at the role of the home in making disciples. But, at this point, we need to see the Scriptural evidence that it is indeed the job and responsibility of fathers to disciple and train their children spiritually, not that of the church.

HOW THE CHURCH CAN HINDER

After reading the last section, you may be thinking "Hey, that is great! But, there are so many dead-beat dads out their today, what are we supposed to do with the kids of those kinds of dads?" Most churches have asked that question and have come to the conclusion that they must be a substitute where the dads are not getting the job done. Before we realized it, the church was handling the training for all dads, Christian and non-Christian alike. But, this is precisely the problem. The church has started doing for the people what was never intended for the church to do in the first place. Many people see it as the responsibility of the preachers and deacons, teachers and elders to teach and disciple the church and to do the work. After all, we pay them to do it. They are the professionals! It is like they say on TV, "Don't try this at home! Let the professionals do it." So, most pastors and church leaders, like me, sigh and resign ourselves to the idea that since fathers are not going to do the work, we will just have to do it for them.

Instead of getting our hands dirty in the hard work of teaching and training, we often want to take the easy way out. In affluent America today, we have decided that we would rather sit and pay for somebody else to go and make disciples. This is the case even when it involves our own children. After all, the schools will teach our children how to read and write. Coach Johnson will show Bobby how to step into the pitch to hit the ball, and Ms. Susie will teach little Molly how to point her toes while doing a pirouette. All we have to do is feed them, clothe them, put a roof over their head, take them on vacation and save enough to get them into a good college. This may sound humorous, but I want us to analyze carefully how we are living and what we expect of the church.

It seems the church has stepped in to do what we don't have time for or the appetite to do ourselves. Many churches today are unknowingly saying to parents, "Just bring your kids to us and we'll keep them out of trouble, give them something to do, show them a good time and do a quick devotion, so you can do what you need to do." As a result, parents drop them off and the church and its staff do the rest. This service is so unbiblical. The church means well, but is hindering the family. Anything the Bible tells us to do that is done for us by staffers in the church, serves to cripple and impair us from doing our part. In the case of training children and leading the family, fathers and mothers must be empowered by the church, not hindered.

As a pastor, I do not want to stand between or in the middle of, a young person and his or her parents in any circumstances. My job is simply to come alongside the family and teach the Word of God and equip them for "works of service." I have come to realize, after studying the Scriptures, not to expect anyone to train or teach my four children spiritually except for me and my wife and I must lead the way. I will answer to God for how I have chosen to be a steward of the gospel in raising godly offspring. When my wife and I stand before Christ, he is not going to ask a pastor or youth minister, "How did you train and teach Katy, Kandace, Clara and Andrew?" He is going to ask us, not the church, because we are responsible and accountable for raising our children in the faith.

Anytime a young person comes and wants to talk to me, as a pastor, I ask them if they have talked to their parents first. Certainly, I'm available to encourage and help, but I never want to be a stumbling block by standing in the place of the parent, principally the father, and his God-given responsibility to raise his children. I have found through the years that some youth leaders feel a sense of pride when the child or young adult comes to them instead of the parent(s) first. These leaders or ministers think they are connecting with the young adult. In actuality, they are hindering the relationship between the parent and the young person. The youth minister can certainly begin a dialog with a young person without the parents' knowledge, but the parents must be made aware of the situation as soon as possible. Of course, exceptions can be made if there are situations that involve abuse or something of that nature.

But what do we do when there is a father in the picture who is not a believer or is unengaged spiritually? What about the young adults who have no family in the church? What do we do about them? To answer these questions, we must return to the teaching of Scripture. We can adopt these young people from these troubled homes into our families. We can mentor them. This may mean inviting them to visit and be with our family and making them feel they are accepted and belong. Paul instructed Titus to teach the elders in Titus 2 that the old should teach, mentor, the young. Pam and I have adopted several young adults through the years and brought them into our family. We try to model and exhibit to them what a biblical family is to look like. We plug them in to our family life. They are a part of what we do at the church. They sit with us and eat meals with us and we try to show them what a Christian family looks like. The most important part of this process is simply to show them love.

Christopher Schlect, in his book, *Critique of Modern Youth Ministry*, (Schlect 2007, 20) says it this way:

> Ministering to children of unbelievers need not be as difficult as it seems. These children should be drawn to associate with Christian families that will "take them in" and mentor them while at church, thereby showing those children the family model as illustrated in the Word of God. Invite them over for dinner, where the Biblical model of the family can be exhibited.

The big question for church leaders is this: *Are we going to continue to lead the church to do the spiritual job that was designed to be done by fathers within the family unit?* Unfortunately, for many churches, this is exactly what is continuing to happen. Collectively, we have been doing this in our mainline and evangelical churches for about four decades. What can be done at this point? Churches must teach the principles of Scripture and make the father and the family responsible.

It is not necessary for us to start ministries for people who will not do what they are called to do themselves. An example of this, where the church does the work, is in a visitation ministry. Why are we comfortable with just a handful of people going out one night a week to visit and evangelize the community? Isn't that what we all are supposed to be doing on a daily basis? We often send money to our state and national organizations to send missionaries out to the mission field for us. This might be good for some situations, but we can and should also be sending forth missionaries from our own church body and partner with our sister churches, as taught in the book of Acts. We can train and equip the body for works of service and not do everything for them. This principle also applies to the training of our young people.

Let us face the facts. Over the last 40 years, we have seen unprecedented numbers of *trained professionals* enter our churches that have been taught to do youth and children's ministry by our seminaries. These are all good, well-meaning people doing the best job they can, still we have seen the largest decline in attendance of young adults in the history of the modern church. We must wake up and realize our burgeoning staffs, bloated budgets, and programs galore are not helping the family raise godly offspring. Instead, even though the attempts are genuine and honest, we are taking the fathers "out at the knees" and hurting the families by trying to do the job for them. There can be some level of success in these programs, but that success has created a perception within the families of our churches that they have been abdicated from their responsibility to raise godly offspring.

Even the way many churches schedule activities during the week serves to fragment and hinder the family. Think about it. The majority of the work of the church is done on weekends and weeknights. This schedule can be so detrimental and actually be a huge hindrance to the functioning of the family. The dad has a meeting Monday night, while the mom has a Bible Study on Tuesday night. There is church on Wednesday night and then the youth group has an outing on Thursday night. Mom and Dad have choir practice on Sunday night, while the kids go to children and youth group functions. Before you know it, the church has monopolized the entire week leaving very little time for families to be together. I know of churches that brag about this kind of active schedule. They say things like, "We sure are busy for the Lord. We've got something going on every night of the week to prove it!" They are not busy for the Lord, rather they are keeping families fragmented, segregated and pulled away from one another.

In their book, *The Family-Friendly Church*, Ben Freudenburg and Rick Lawrence describe how the church should help families. They write (Freudenburg and Lawrence, 82-83):

> We often ask homes to sacrifice themselves to keep the church organization healthy and functioning. Rather, we should ask the church to sacrifice its business priorities to keep the home healthy and functional. When was the last time you went to a congregational meeting to answer the question, "How do we help struggling homes?" rather than "How do we make our church better?" We call for emergency meetings to strategize about financial shortfalls but not to strategize about helping a church member in crisis. It's a question of where to invest our limited time and energy. Are we really about the business of building bigger, better church organizations, or are we focused on building the church through the homes where people live?

Why did Jesus come? I don't believe he came to build better synagogues. He spent quite a bit of time giving critical instruction to the leaders of "the church" of that day. Jesus came to build better people. We know he didn't come to be served; he came to pour himself out as a servant to others. He's the model for the church. We must ask ourselves if our church structures are serving the very people Jesus came to save. If our homes are falling apart and we're pulling families in a myriad of directions with tons of functions and activities, then we've effectively missed the boat. We must stop weakening our families by tying up so much of their time.

Hence, the question arises. *When does a family have time to be a family and do any teaching and training?* The answer is that most do not. That is why teachers, coaches, computers, video games, and the TV are raising most of our kids. It is the worldview and agenda of these people and things that are influencing our children the most. There will be much more on this dilemma in the next chapter. The church must stop being an accomplice in the crime of *family fragmentation.* We must be bold enough and wise enough to look at our scheduling and free up time for the family.

I know even in saying all of this, some will say, "But, most families aren't going to sit at home studying their Bibles and singing *Kum Bah Yah* every night of the week." I am well aware of that fact, too. Many families will simply choose to do other things with their time instead of teaching and training their children in the ways of the Lord. But, knowing that is the case doesn't mean that we have to occupy all the families of the church because a few will not participate in the spiritual home education of their children. We must hold up the standard of what the Scriptures teach. The Bible clearly says in Deuteronomy 6:7 that we are to teach the commands of God in this fashion: "You shall teach them diligently to your children, and shall talk of them when you sit in your house, and when you walk by the way, and when you lie down, and when you rise." If the family is never together and never at home, how can this possibly be accomplished? God help us to become "family-friendly" in our churches. It is imperative that we clear some nights so that families have time to be families, whether they choose to utilize this time or not. Some will and those families that do will benefit greatly from their investment.

This process of simplification will not be easy. It is much like trying to turn a large ship on a dime. The ship I'm speaking of is the youth industry. Having been a youth pastor previously, I still receive all the mail for the youth pastor. It is literally three-fourths of my mail. There are books, concerts, Bible studies, camps, games, retreats, programs, music, seminars, conferences, symposiums, conventions, and on and on. LifeWay Christian Resources (the

Southern Baptist Convention's publication hub) has annual sales approaching $500 million with a huge chunk of that being children and youth resources marketed to churches. This is a massive industry! As most people know or are aware, there are many speakers who are full time on the youth speaking circuit. Musicians, comedians and evangelists perform from city to city before huge crowds of young people. But what has all of this gotten us? Where has this taken us?

We already know the statistics. Our young adults continue to walk away in droves. In fact, many of them are already gone, even though they may sit in our churches Sunday after Sunday. They have already checked out, because they have no purpose nor do they see the relevance for even being in our churches. Ken Ham and Britt Beemer address this phenomenon in their book, *Already Gone*. Writes Ham and Beemer (Ham and Beemer, 28):

> Yes, look to the left and look to the right this Sunday. Put down your church bulletin; look at those kids and imagine that two-thirds of them aren't even there. Why? Because they are already gone. It's time to wake up and see the tidal wave washing away the foundation of your church. The numbers are in—and they don't look good. From across Christendom the reports are the same: A mass exodus is underway. Most youth of today will not be coming to church tomorrow. Nationwide polls and denominational reports are showing that the next generation is calling it quits on the traditional church. And it's not just happening on the nominal fringe; it's happening at the core of the faith.

It is time to get young people out of our game rooms and get them plugged into our churches and get them on the mission field of life. We need to see our young adults as capable of "being about the Father's business." We need to expect them to step up to the level of a teenage apostle or Timothy or David.

Does offering more concerts, camps, lock-ins, pizza blasts, zip-lines, ski trips, and the like stand to give us spiritually mature young adults? No, not if that's all we give them. A steady diet of activities and fun is not what they need or want. Our society's youth orientation has bred little more than young adults hyped up on the junk food of entertainment and fun, yet they are starving to death and dying for answers to the difficult and tough questions of the day. Our young people sit in our churches week after week and we see them, but are they really there? Are they really engaged? Do they want to be at church or are they just coming because they have to or because they've been lured by the fun and games? Doesn't our focus need to change?

Wonderfully, over the last few years, I've started to see a change and it's beginning in our seminaries. The wonderful thing about that is the change will spread more rapidly to our churches. Here is an example. In 2006, Southern Baptist Seminary changed its entire philosophy and focus regarding youth ministry. The leadership decided to equip their students to focus on and help the family versus focusing on just the youth. Seminary President Al Mohler is credited with having the vision to move the seminary and its focus to being family-centered in its teaching and training of students. More and more seminaries are beginning to train Family Ministers instead of Youth Ministers. I may be splitting hairs to some, but even using the term *youth* versus *young adults* has become an important distinction to make. The word youth connotes the homogenization of our young people into one large amoeba that has been *segregated* from the body. The words young adults connote young people who have been *integrated* into the body. Youth groups do things alone. Young adults do things with adults.

If you think about it, of all the programs in churches which one is most commonly the largest and well funded? The answer: youth programs. It seems that evangelical churches, and many mainline churches, began breaking out the youth in their congregations about 30-40 years ago. In fact, there is a feeling in Christendom that you aren't doing too well as a church if you can't fund and hire at least a part-time youth minister of some sort. But, what do youth ministries do? Many of these programs, if not managed carefully, can breed immaturity because they hinder younger people from associating with and learning from their elders. Paul told young Timothy to "flee youthful lusts" (2 Tim. 2:22). Yet, it is common to take the young adults on an outing at night and we have to station chaperones throughout the church bus to make sure everyone is being nice. Is that something we should have to be doing with adults in the church? There should never be a youth function in a church in which everyone, young and old alike, cannot participate. When we go skiing at our church, anyone can come along. When we go ride bikes, any member of the body can and should be allowed to attend. All ages like to have fun and all ages need sound Bible teaching.

IDENTITY CRISIS

Many young adults, after they leave our youth programs, have little or no identity apart from the youth group. A transition from youth group to the adult church seldom occurs. Many young people leave our youth programs and they don't feel they have a place in the church. Often, they feel kicked out of the youth program. Some even ask to come back and be a part of the youth group even when they enter college. They do so because they are being asked to leave the fun and games and move into "big" church, where they believe it's dry, dull and excruciatingly boring. They may have seldom been in the adult church services, so they have little or no idea what being an adult church member is all about.

When we totally separate our young adults from the rest of the church body, we are setting them up for an identity crisis. They don't know who they are apart from their friends and buddies in the youth group. They know nothing of the functioning of the church, as a whole, outside of their youth room. After all, they have their own culture and music, geared to their own tastes. So, by the time they are 18 and we tell them they must leave our youth groups, they are sent to the grown up church where, in some cases many have never been. It is culture shock to say the least!

Despite all of this, some may think that we are trying to take the fun out of the lives of our young adults. Some say, "They've got to be kids. Let them have a little fun." Please understand, I am not against anyone having fun, but is this the role of the church? Are we supposed to set up our churches to be centers for having fun? Somehow we think teenagers are entitled to more fun than anybody else in the church. We feel we must put something fun on the calendar every week or two, certainly monthly, so they can have a good time. Do we owe any group in the church a good time? Many youth ministries seem to be run like a cruise ship. We hear things like, "When's the next event? What are we eating, pizza or hotdogs?" No wonder we have such a high turnover rate with youth ministers. It is easy to burn out after two or three years of this kind of activity planning.

Can youth groups be a negative influence on our young people? Sure they can. We place our young people in these peer-driven groups where the spiritual maturity is usually very low and yet we desire for them to grow spiritually. How? How can they grow spiritually in these environments? Most of the time, youth pastors are trying to administrate some sort of crowd control versus being able to really teach. Unfortunately, our young people tend to find their identity in their friends or what they wear, drive or have. Some young people have their entire identity wrapped up in the type of clothes they wear, cell phone they carry and who they are dating. This same mentality often transfers into our youth groups and can even be fed within the youth group.

Through the years, I've become more and more dismayed that we no longer mix our young people with our adults in our churches in any way. We keep our youth in their own rooms, as far away from everyone else in the church as possible, in case they get too loud or rowdy. We let them paint the walls tie-dyed, put up posters of Christian musicians, many of whom honestly look like leftovers from the 70's group *KISS*, and bring in sofas for them to lounge on while they play video games and hang out. Some youth rooms I've seen look more like arcades. Some churches have even given their youth their own building, where they come for an entertainment smorgasbord anytime they want. Is this the structural model we really believe is going to grow mature, solid, faith-filled, Christ-centered, young adults? We must stop kidding ourselves. The numbers, the surveys, and the statistical data do not lie. Many of our young adults continue to abandon their faith and will continue to do so unless we change our strategy and return to a Biblical model.

THE POWER OF MENTORSHIP

We have forgotten something in our churches today that once was a powerful tool and still can be: *mentorship*. For years, even in our secular culture, one had to become an apprentice before he could work a job as a craftsman within a trade. He had to be trained and equipped by an elder who was seasoned, experienced and knowledgeable. The same is true in the church. Churches should work to promote *cross-generational interaction* as Paul admonished Titus to teach the elders in Titus 2. In separating the youth from the church body at large, we are in essence saying, "Unlike adults, they can't handle the weighty things of Scripture." It is okay for us to give them a driver's license at 16 and put them behind the wheel of a 5,000 pound vehicle and turn them loose on our highways. We expect them to learn algebra, chemistry and calculus. Certainly, they can study and learn Scripture as well. Our young people need to be with adults and be trained older to younger. In fact, they will graduate from high school and college and go to work in environments with people of all ages. Only in our schools and churches are our young adults segregated by age. Remember, Paul mentored young Timothy, who was likely in his teens or early twenties. Paul poured his life into Timothy (see 1 and 2 Timothy) and we should be doing the same for young people in our churches.

This practice is much more effective than youth programs at large, which are mostly peer driven.

The power of mentorship and the mentorship process is a fundamental ingredient in becoming what we would consider a ROP church. This is a Scriptural model that will have a major emphasis on training and preparing the next generation to carry the teachings of Christ. If we can't get the gospel to the next generation by properly handing off our faith in Chris, then the church will become impotent and useless. It doesn't matter what we do with budgets, mission statements, planning committees, and the like. If we don't transfer our faith in Christ to the next generation, Christianity in America will go the way of Europe. Many of Europe's beautiful churches have now been turned into pubs, bike shops and municipal buildings.

You can now see that ROP is truly more of a *way of thinking and living* rather than a program. Are you starting to catch the vision? The church is to help and partner with the family to grow our young adults in the way of the Lord. We are partners with the family in training our young adults. Again, we don't do the job for the parents, but partner with them. The church's vision must shift from a consumer-driven focus regarding our young people, to a partner-driven focus. In other words, the church must stop seeing itself as a vending machine of fun activities to give young people or children something to do to keep them out of trouble. As parents, we must stop seeing the church as a place where we drop off the kids to let the pastors train them or give them a little faith development. This consumer mentality, where we come to church and feed ourselves at the "program" feeding trough, needs to change.

We must return to the Scriptural mandate that the older should teach and train the younger. We must stop thinking the church *building* and its *programs* are the conduits through which the gospel is spread. The gospel is spread through *people*, not programs. What programs existed in the first church? None that I know of with the exception of meeting together to fellowship, break bread, study the gospel and pray (see Acts 2:42-47). Afterwards, they left each other's homes and went out into their community and shared Jesus. The gospel must travel house by house through the community in the same way it did 2,000 years ago. If we want to have programs, why don't we set them up to follow the principles outlined in Scripture?

MAKING HOME THE HUB

We have this mistaken idea that the church is the hub and the families should plug into the church and its programs. Yet, we have it backwards. The home is the hub through which we disseminate the gospel. The church is the equipping center, while the home should be the evangelization center. The Scripture teaches in Ephesians 4:11-16, the church and its pastor/teachers "equip the body" to do the work of the ministry. So, the church is the place we come to be equipped. We do so on the Lord's Day and then we go out and share the gospel throughout the week. After all, we must get the "salt" out of the shaker if we are going to be the salt of the earth. The church is the place where we come together and get our marching orders and then we go. We must go and live out our faith by making our homes "ministry centers." The church is to train and equip families to become "hospitality" and "ministry centers" where the discipleship of the children takes place at the same time we're reaching our communities and the world in making disciples of all nations.

The first church is our example. The people met in each other's homes and they went out and "added to their number daily." People were coming to Christ on a daily basis. How were they doing that? They were leading people to Jesus Christ in *their homes*. Can you imagine that? They weren't expecting the pastor, deacons or Sunday school teachers to do the work of leading the community to Jesus. They were doing this *home by home* and *family by family*. As pastors, we have inadvertently trained our people to be ambulances for the gospel. They bring the lost to the hospital for the sin-sick, where the professionals, the doctors of the spirit, will treat and fix them.

Why do we come to church? What is the purpose? Is it to see people come to Christ? Certainly this is the first step in the process and arguably the most important, but shouldn't we seek to follow the example of the first church? They were leading people to Christ during the week, and then introducing them to the church family on the Lord's Day. Hebrews 10:24-25: "And let us consider how to stir up one another to love and good works, not neglecting to meet together, as is the habit of some, but encouraging one another, and all the more as you see the Day drawing near." We should come together to encourage and equip and then go make disciples! We've got to train our people to be paramedics with the life-giving gospel of Jesus Christ instead of ambulances just carrying people to church. We must go to people. A wonderful way to reach others is simply to get them into our homes and show them Christian hospitality. Is your home a ministry center of hospitality? Is it a hub for the gospel or a dead-end spoke in the wheel? Our young people need to see Christianity in action. For too long we have ministered "to" our children, instead of teaching them to minister for Christ. What better way to model ministry than for them to see us ministering in our homes.

CHILDREN IN THE MEETING

Our church doesn't have a youth pastor, children's pastor, children's church, or a nursery. We want and desire everyone to be together. We believe the Bible teaches we are one body in Christ. This concept of one body is important because it encompasses all Christians of all ages. This is a view of ROP that one might miss. If we aren't careful, we will view ROP as just something you do with a teen, but it is so much more. As I shared earlier, ROP is a process or a way of thinking that begins when a child is born. Truly, from the moment a child is born and entrusted to his or her parents, the job of teaching and training that child begins. We teach our children things as elementary as holding a fork or drinking from a cup and progress to how to handle money and become responsible. We don't wait to teach children how to hold a fork until they are eight or nine. That would be too late by anyone's estimation. The same is true for our children spiritually. We must begin teaching them when they are very young. In this way, ROP really begins when a child is born. How can the church assist in this process? What do we do with the children?

To begin to answer these questions, let's look at how Jesus interacted with the children and how he taught them. When Jesus taught and delivered his sermon on the mountain, did he teach just the parents? Did Jesus tell Peter, James and John to take the children down to the bottom of the hill and play with them or have a children's church, so he could teach, without distraction, at the top of the hill? Did Jesus ever do this on any occasion? Not that I can find in Scripture. How about the Apostle Paul? We should look closely at his writings, since he wrote extensively to the churches. How did he write his letters? Take for instance the Ephesians 6 passage where he addresses the children in verse one and then just three verses later the fathers. Were the children siphoned off somewhere else when the letter was being read to the believers in Ephesus? No, they were all together.

I am not a Greek scholar, but I have spoken at length with those who know the original language of the New Testament to help me understand how Paul wrote to the churches in his epistles. I am told he often used what is called the "vocative case." For instance, in the Ephesians 6 passage just mentioned, the "vocative case" is used as Paul addresses both the children and the fathers. The vocative case is the case of direct address. It is used when one person is speaking to another, calling out or saying their name, or generally addressing them in a way that leaves no question as to whether that person is being addressed. This indicates when Paul wrote his letters, he expected those being addressed to be in the meeting and hear the reading of the letter. Paul wrote his letter to the church at Ephesus fully anticipating and expecting that the children would hear what was directly being addressed to them.

This means the children were included in the church meeting and they were physically present in that church meeting. This fact seems almost strange in our day and age when, in many churches, we send our children off to children's church to eat snacks, color and watch videos. Yet, as we study the Scriptures, we can not find any verses in the Bible where the children were pulled out of the meeting. It would have been completely unorthodox to do so. There is *never* a time or an instance in Scripture when the children were separated from the parents/family when the people of God met together. At this point, I'm reminded of Jesus and his rebuke of the disciples for not allowing the children to come to him recorded in Mark 10:13-14:

> *And they were bringing children to him that he might touch them, and the disciples rebuked them. But when Jesus saw it, he was indignant and said to them, "Let the children come to me; do not hinder them, for to such belongs the kingdom of God."*

I know for many churches, the idea of having young children in our services is very counter-cultural. Many church leaders and members say the children are too noisy and disruptive and people can't worship the Lord. Yet, when we say these things, we are much like the disciples when they tried to shoo away the children. Consequently, in our day, we have lost the blessing of the full body being together in the meeting. Sadly, we have become comfortable with some of the body missing. How have we gotten to this point? The church wasn't this way 40 to 50 years ago. It has happened, because it's convenient. Many years ago, it would have been unheard of to have a nursery in the church. Ask someone that went to church in this nation in the 1950s or 1960s. There were very few, if any nurseries in our churches, until well after WWII, when many women entered the workforce. Yet today, we would rather not be bothered with children, ours or someone else's, because they may make noise in the service or can be disruptive. However, pulling the children out of our meetings was simply not a normative practice in Scripture.

When we go to a restaurant, there is not a place for the children to go sit and eat by themselves with people to help them cut up their food and feed them. So, what do we do when we go out to eat and order food for our children? We go through the process and the inconvenience of cutting their food for them into bite-size portions. We teach our children how to behave in a restaurant. If we go to the movie theater, there isn't a section of the theater where we send the children to watch the movie with other children, while someone else watches them for us. No, we take care of our children and teach them how to be quiet and listen during the movie. We help them through this *season* of their lives. I call it a season because it will quickly pass and we'll wonder where the time has gone. The same is true at ball games, concerts, recitals and the like. We are with our children and we help them. We teach them. So, why do we hesitate to do so at church? We can just as easily help the children digest the meeting or service, just as we would help them with cutting their spaghetti into bite-size pieces at a restaurant or even at a meal at home.

We should want our children to experience being in the presence of the Lord, being taught by a shepherd in the church. I know that I want my children to experience everything in the meeting of our people. Children miss so much when they are in a room somewhere watching a video, eating snacks. They miss seeing the Body worship together. My children experience seeing people raising their hands in praise to the Lord as they lift their voices in song. They get to hear testimonies of those that have come to Christ. They see people weeping under the conviction of the Holy Spirit. They see fathers praying over their families. They get to hear the Word of God taught by men whom the entire church trusts to teach them. Why shouldn't the children hear this teaching corporately as well? Why should this job be handed off to someone else in another place in the church? Certainly, there are always reservations. Children are messy. They talk out loud. They cry and make noises. Well, you name it and they'll do it. Yet, over time something wonderful happens. They learn. Yes, they learn to listen and be still and, oh do they listen! They are sponges taking in all that the Body gets to see and hear. Those experiences will stay with them for a lifetime.

I can share a personal example of this process. My family has had the privilege of adopting two children from China, a girl and a boy. When we brought Andrew, our son, home from China he was three-years-old. We got him home to America on a Thursday and we had him in church on Sunday. He couldn't speak a word of English. In fact, he could barely speak any Chinese. He had never been out of the orphanage in China until two weeks prior to meeting us. He had never been in a car, a bus and certainly not on a plane. He was taken out of everything he knew and thrust into a brand-new, frightening world. He had club feet and numerous other health issues that had not yet been addressed. Yet, we had him in church on Sunday, four days after his arrival in the U.S. and if that wasn't enough, we had him on the front row! (That's where my family and I sit in church every Sunday.)

Do you want to know how he did that first Sunday? He was terrible! No, he was worse than that. He was *absolutely awful!* He talked out loud! Chinese at that! He crawled on the floor, under the chairs, on us; you name it, and he did it. Was it embarrassing? Yes. And the same was true when we brought Clara home as a one-year-old, three years earlier. But, the church welcomes children and understands this behavior as being a part of the learning process. The next Sunday Andrew struggled again, but he was learning. Slowly but surely, he was learning how to act as we taught him. By the fourth week, you couldn't even tell he was in the building. In just one month, you couldn't even tell he was there. What happened? He had been trained and taught to know what to do and how to act in church. He still has moments of restlessness, as all children (and even some adults do); however, he usually listens very well to the teaching.

A child will learn anything in life when we make up our mind and *decide* to teach them. It doesn't matter if they are three-years-old and from a foreign country or if they are any age where they can reason and think. It seems around the age of four years old, most parents don't have a choice but to train their child to be a part of the church. Most churches tell parents their children can no longer come to the nursery at that age. So, it seems many children learn to behave in church at age four, unless there is a children's church. If there is children's church, they get a few more years segregated from the *Body* until they must learn to be a part of the church family. Yet, at some point in time, we teach the children what to do in church. Sooner or later, they learn. Children are a *blessing* of a growing church, not a *nuisance*. The Bible says in Psalm 127:3-5a:

> *Behold, children are a heritage from the LORD, the fruit of the womb a reward. Like arrows in the hand of a warrior are the children of one's youth. Blessed is the man who fills his quiver with them!*

I love the wording of the King James Version of Mark 10:14 that we looked at earlier. The verse in the KJV begins: "Suffer the little children to come unto me…" I am grateful for a church that is literally willing to *suffer* for the children. Why should a church do so and what does this have to do with ROP? A church should allow families to worship together a part of the *one* family. Churches have the opportunity to tell the body (a family of families) that all are welcome at the Lord's Table, even our youngest. A ROP church exemplifies this idea. For most, seeing church life in this way is a total paradigm shift and would be a significant change in philosophy, church culture and practice. Again, ROP is not just a program, ceremony or ritual to be completed at a specific age (although the ceremony itself is a one-time event). ROP embodies biblical patterns that become carefully woven through the fabric of the entire church family.

TRAINING DISCIPLES TO MAKE DISCIPLES

As we continue to look at what the church can do to help families, please know that I'm not going to suggest you buy a workbook, or attend a conference or travel to a three-day retreat. The church should be creating an atmosphere and a culture where we train the body of disciples to go out and make disciples. We get this mandate from Acts 2. Remember according to Jesus, the ultimate goal is to make disciples of all nations. So, as churches, shouldn't we be teaching and training our people to be disciple-makers? Think of all the time Jesus spent teaching and training. It would be interesting to know how much time, cumulatively speaking, it took in Jesus' life to perform all the miracles versus the time it took him to teach and to train his disciples. I think one could safely say Jesus spent the majority of his ministry time teaching and training. We see the Apostle Paul also doing so with Timothy, Titus, Barnabas and Silas.

If disciple-making is this important, then we must ask ourselves if we are getting the job done. Are we succeeding in equipping our young people and giving them an appetite for God's Word? We must teach and preach the Word of God and explain it to them in a way that they desire to study it for themselves. We must help people become students of the Word of God. John tells us Jesus is the "word" that became flesh and dwelled among us. Indeed, when we fall in love with the Word of God, the Bible, we literally love Jesus, because he is the "Word." Many people, particularly our young people, seem to be Biblically illiterate, because they seldom read the Bible. They may read a few verses from a devotional book in the morning or evening before they go to bed, but not really study the Bible. Our lack of spiritual depth as the Body of Christ is primarily because most don't study the Bible. We are to be a workman who doesn't need to be ashamed and who correctly handles the word of truth (see 2 Tim. 2:15). Most people just read a verse for the day or hurry through some Bible reading plan, while never truly studying the Bible. So, we are spiritually anemic at best, or dying a slow death, at worst.

I am convinced one of the most important things I can do as a pastor is to inspire people to read the Bible. I thoroughly believe to the degree that our congregations are studying the Scriptures as Bereans (see Acts 17:11) is the degree we will grow in our faith and knowledge in the Lord. Just as water and sunlight cause the plant to grow, so too will the Christian who studies the Word of God consistently and diligently. In 2 Timothy 3:14-16, the Apostle Paul encourages Timothy to continue in what he has learned since he was a child.

> *But as for you, continue in what you have learned and have firmly believed, knowing from whom you learned it and how from childhood you have been acquainted with the sacred writings, which are able to make you wise for salvation through faith in Christ Jesus. All Scripture is breathed out by God and profitable for teaching, for reproof, for correction, and for training in righteousness, that the man of God may be competent, equipped for every good work.*

Are we teaching the Bible to our children? We should be. What is the purpose for Scripture and what is its use? Paul tells Timothy Scripture is to be used for: teaching, reproof, correction and training in righteousness. Why? So, we will become equipped for every good work. If we are equipped, then we can truly call ourselves disciples. But, if we are not equipped and we are not students of the Bible, then we aren't disciples. We are only spectators who need to get out of our seats and into the spiritual "gym" and get to work. Many believers are lazy and undisciplined when it comes to Bible study and this is evident in the way we are living. I realize the most obvious method that most families rely on today for teaching the Bible to children and young people is Sunday school. Yet, as we will discuss in detail in the next chapter, Bible study should not be limited to age-segregated Sunday school; but should be centered in the home. As has been described, there is so much that younger Christians can and should learn from seasoned, older Christians as modeled in Titus 2.

Please hear my heart. The purpose of this book is not to explain ROP to you like one would a diet or some sort of fad. ROP may sound new because of the term or phrase in that it is unfamiliar. But, the principles of ROP are from the Word of God and have existed for centuries. The foundation of our lives must be built upon the authority of the Word of God, not a program or new spiritual fad. The Bible must be the foundation from which we build our lives, our children and our churches. What I'm attempting to do is awaken within us what we already know intuitively, but perhaps just need to be reminded.

GIVE THEM A JOB

Everyone likes to be needed. When we aren't part of something, or aren't involved, then we don't feel needed. One of the areas where the church struggles today is plugging in our young adults. We, the church, must do all we can to integrate our young men and women into every facet of church life. Remember, Jesus was 12 years old when he had to "be about his Father's business." So, why not include our 12-year-olds in the adult choir? Why shouldn't we be training and mentoring them in the various functions of the church (the Father's business)? Certainly an older soprano in the choir can teach and mentor a younger soprano or an older bass can teach a younger bass. We do this at our church and it's amazing to see the ownership the young adults have when they have a part or stake in what goes on at the church. The bond that grows between the older teacher and the young apprentice is special as well. When a young person has a job or responsibility, they feel they belong, then the church is no longer just their parent's church. They say, "It's my church." You will hear them say, "I get to sing in the choir at my church." It becomes "my" church instead of just a place they are made to go.

We allow our young adults to serve on most of our committees as apprentices. They can be ushers and greeters, help teach children's Sunday school classes and work on local and even international mission projects. Young adults are allowed to attend adult Sunday school classes, read Scripture during the worship service, lead in prayer, help run the audio/visual equipment for services, work in Vacation Bible School, volunteer to serve meals to shut-ins, go on missions trips with other adults, visit nursing homes, play in the church praise band, plan and lead worship, etc.

Let me state at this point: young people are not to become substitutes for adults. We recognize they are indeed young adults and they need training and mentoring. Rather, they are essential, complementary components to our more seasoned adults. Again, what we have implemented is what we see in that great mentoring passage in Titus 2. We work very hard to provide activities that allow participation with adults and in family-oriented settings. The goal is not to group the young adults together for play and entertainment. Doing so only reinforces to them that they have an identity separate from the rest of the adult community. I'm not saying God can't work in youth group settings. However, I'm convinced the Scriptural path of mentoring and giving our young people a stake in their church is a better way to accomplish the goal of raising Christ-centered young adults and easing the transition between childhood and adulthood.

Changing the Culture in the Church

Today, we are involved in a war for the hearts, souls, and minds of our children and our families. I believe the church is failing to transmit her religious heritage to the next generation. Sermons in many of our churches are now more "therapeutic" than instructional. Our worship services have become grounded more in what we feel than in what we know and understand about Scripture. In many cases we have stopped training and discipling our people.

Why is it that the church, in many instances, no longer represents the power of the action of God in the world? We have compromised the Gospel of Jesus Christ. The church has quit training and evangelizing and it is literally dying a slow death in America. This slow death is akin to the proverbial frog in the kettle that slowly has the temperature turned up so that the tepid water eventually boils him to death. We are being boiled to death by entertainment, "spectatorism" and a cheap, prosperity gospel. church attendance continues to drop and we have forgotten the goal of advancing God's Kingdom on earth, instead of our kingdom. The purpose of the church is to be God's missionary people in the world. We are to be adding disciples to the flock, not just fattening those that are already in the flock with entertainment, and fun and games that offer little substance each week.

For many in the current generation, the church is seen as fractured, segregated, watered-down, and devoid of any cultural relevancy. What passes for Christianity and true discipleship in many of our churches is often just a faint shadow of what the Scriptures actually teach and admonish the church to be. The typical teen in an American church feels little or no sense of ownership in their church simply because they do not feel they are a part of that church.

My prayer is the church will get back to being the one church and function as a complete Body again. Leaders, I want to encourage you to involve your young adults in the church. Discourage peer association at times when the worship service is taking place if it is deterring their discipleship or ability to listen and learn. It is sometimes necessary to discourage young adults from going to the back of the church and sitting together slumped down in their seats. Encourage families to sit together. There is plenty of time to socialize with friends before or after the service. What is the purpose for being at church in the first place? It's to be trained and equipped while being edified and encouraged.

If you have a youth ministry at your church, or you are a youth leader, seek to embrace the facilitator role described earlier, as a minister to the family. No longer should you see yourself in the role of having responsibility for raising young adults, instead seek to get the message across to the parents that you are transferring this responsibility back to them. A good intermediate step (we are doing this at our church) is to have parent/child Bible Studies or Sunday school classes (we call them "mentoring" classes). The youth minister can begin these classes, but gradually hand them off to the parents. Again, if there are activities to be planned like an outing to go ski or ride bikes, plan it as a church-wide activity. We don't have a youth committee at our church. We have a family committee. We plan activities for the family that will reach out and impact other families in our community. It is important to get outside of our four walls and no longer just tithe to ourselves, but spend that money on reaching people. Everyone needs to be involved in that process and that certainly includes our young adults.

REDIRECTING OUR FOCUS

When one looks at how the typical church ministers today, could it be that we have placed the majority of our attention and money in the wrong place? For many churches, the children and youth ministries receive the biggest chunk of ministry budget dollars, while ministries to train and equip men receive almost nothing. I mention the men, because they are the fathers that have been given the Scriptural mandate (Eph. 6:4) to lead in bringing up the children in the discipline and instruction of the Lord. Because of this mandate shouldn't we focus more on the fathers? I know many dads don't even come to church today or they are not involved in their children's lives. Unfortunately, this is a common occurrence. That is why we have so many women who have to teach, serve on our committees and do much of the work of the church. Many might say, "Why bother with ministering to the fathers?"

To begin to answer this question, we need to briefly go back and look at some history. I think most would agree we have seen the total breakdown and decimation of the moral fiber of this nation in the last 50 years. Most would agree the church in America is in decline, in almost lock-step with the nation. Many would agree the family is broken in America as well. In review, our nation has become morally decadent, the church has become mostly ineffective and families have been ripped apart at the seams over the last several decades in this nation. Why? Where does the blame lie? Should the blame lie with the children? Should we blame the mothers? Should we blame the fathers? Let's return to Scripture. God told Abraham in Genesis 18:19, that he must "command his children and his household to keep the way of the Lord by doing righteousness and justice." In Psalm 78 the fathers are told to teach the commandments of God so the next generation might know them, even the children yet to be born. Fathers are to tell the commands to their children, so that "they should set their hope in God and not forget the works of God ..." (see Ps. 78: 5-6). Is this happening today? I think not. Therefore, according to Scripture, we have a *father problem* in our homes, churches and nation.

Fathers have not been trained and equipped. They have forgotten or don't even know how to pass on the commands of God to the next generation. Many lament and say we have a youth problem in America. I believe we have a family problem that stems because we have fathers that are not doing the job they have been commanded to do. The church has stopped reaching fathers. Can you see that in your own church? Somehow over the years, those of us in the church have missed this. We've been doing ministry to the children and the youth and we have forgotten the fathers.

It has been said, "As the father goes, so goes the family. As the family goes, so goes the church and as the church goes, so goes a nation." We all know or have at least heard 2 Chronicles 7:14 many times. "If my people who are called by my name humble themselves, and pray and seek my face and turn from their wicked ways, then I will hear from heaven and will forgive their sin and heal their land." I recognize we often quote this passage out of context, because it is a promise to the nation of Israel, but the principle still applies. God's people must turn from their "wicked ways." Who leads in this? I know this is dangerous to say, in an ever increasing egalitarian society, but the fathers are commanded to lead, if we believe the Bible. It's that simple.

Adam was created first by God and then Eve from Adam's rib to be his "suitable helper." Husbands are called to be the head of the wife as Christ is the head of the church (see Eph. 5:21-33). Please understand, the father and husband is to be a servant leader who is willing to submit his own will to that of the Father and therefore be willing to die to himself. When he dies to himself, he is willing to give up his own life and die for his wife. Yet many fathers and husbands aren't leading today. In many homes we see mixed-up roles where the mother is leading instead of the father. Yet, the ladies are only trying to fill the vacuum left by the men in the home and the church.

Review almost any research study that's been done when it comes to the issue of the importance of the father's role in the home and you will find: *It is the religious practice of the father that most greatly determines the future attendance or absence from the church of the children* (see barna.org).The fact that homes with dedicated and engaged fathers work best may be politically incorrect, but they simply confirm what psychologists, criminologists, educationalists, and traditional Christians know. You cannot buck the biology of the created order.

We know a mother's role will always remain primary in terms of intimacy, care, and nurture. It's still true some of the toughest men I know still sport a tattoo dedicated to the love of his mother, without the slightest embarrassment or sentimentality. No father can replace that relationship. But it is equally true that when a child begins to move into that period of differentiation from the home and engagement with the world, he or she looks increasingly to the father for his role model. Where the father is indifferent, inadequate, or just plain absent, that task of differentiation and engagement is much harder. When children see that church is a "women and children" thing, they will respond accordingly, by not going to church or going much less. I've seen this most recently in doing mission work in Mexico. Most of the churches are filled with women and children, but no men or boys, primarily because the males feel religion is for women and children.

Now I realize some of you reading this will say, "This is a utopian ideal. It sounds good, but it's not practical for my situation or my church." I understand your sentiment. I truly do. The Bible clearly presents as "normative" the truth that fathers are to be the spiritual leaders in the home. I understand we are ministering in a society today that is increasingly unfaithful in spiritual and physical relationships. There is a huge number of single-parent families and a complexity of step-relationships in our nation. Many men are itinerant figures at best in the home. There are potentially many women reading this book who are doing their very best to be father and mother in the home. I tell you dear lady, don't lose hope. God will provide and he will take care of you and your children. You can see as a wonderful encouragement the example of Lois and Eunice, the grandmother and mother of Timothy and how they trained him without the father being engaged in his spiritual upbringing (see 2 Tim. 1:5-6, Acts 16:1). So, as churches, we don't neglect you and your plight. We must come alongside and help. I try to provide a male influence in the lives of many young men and ladies in our church who do not have a father in the home. There are other men in the church who do the same. Certainly, this is very difficult and there is much that could be said here. However, my purpose is not to address the exceptions, but rather the rule of Scripture in this matter of reaching and equipping the fathers. Again, this endeavor is also difficult and it takes much time and attention to draw the men to Christ. But, are we attempting to do so or have we just given up?

It seems many churches across America have accepted fatherlessness as the norm, and even the ideal in some cases. Today we have emasculated or gender-free Bibles and there is a growing movement toward egalitarian doctrine that is feminizing the church. Yet, we cannot feminize the church and keep the men and we cannot keep the children, if we do not keep the men. No father equals no family and no family eventually equals no faith. Winning and keeping men is essential to the community of faith and vital to the work of all mothers and the future salvation of our children. So, how can we shift our focus?

Understanding the need to grow our men and reach out to others in our community, we started a group called Iron Men. The Bible teaches in Proverbs 27:17, "Iron sharpens iron, and one man sharpens another." Under this premise, we began the ministry with only a handful of guys, but in less than a year we were averaging around 50 men each week. We continue to meet every Wednesday at 12-noon for lunch at a local Cowboy Church (a large building in the middle of our town with plenty of tables and chairs). I bring in lunch, and I put out a donation basket for those who wish to give and with what is given each week, the cost to the church per man, per week is only $1.

I have seen this ministry literally change the lives of many men and their families. I could tell you story after story about men who have been coming to these meetings getting *sharpened* each week. What kind of impact has it had on their families? I wish I could show you a video of these guys giving testimony to the changes they are seeing in their families because they have decided to allow Jesus Christ to be their Lord and their boss. It's phenomenal!

We must begin reaching men again, not to the exclusion of women, but the family rises and falls with the leadership, or the lack thereof, of men. It is God's created order and his design. We must return to this design and recognize within the church that our role is to partner with men and families to train and educate the young. As we understand our responsibility and our role as a church in doing so, we will reach families in ways that we're not currently doing. Think of the investment for only $1. In a year's period of time the church will have about $3,000 invested in this ministry, which is just a "drop in the bucket" compared to many of our other ministries.

The Role of the Home
in Making Disciples

MY STRUGGLE-MY REVELATION

As I begin to type the words to this chapter, I sit in my small office in my basement and I look around at it and its contents. It has a small desk, a chair, a book case and a filing cabinet. It has some Christmas wrapping paper, a few boxes and my golf clubs that haven't been used in almost four years. My little office has a small table with an old fax machine on it and about a dozen, small, framed pictures of various members of my family. There is a picture of all the children when they were small. There's a picture of my grandmother, who has gone to be with the Lord and another one of me and Pam when we were first married twenty years ago. There is also a picture of me singing with a quartet that I sang with for about ten years. As I look at those pictures and think about those days that are in my past and I think about where I am today, writing this book, I'm struck with a sobering thought: *I can't go back*.

Have you ever had that thought? I guess we all have at one time or another. We know we can't go back and relive another day. When the day is gone, it is gone. Knowing that is good and bad. There are so many things I wish I could go back and do over. We've all said it: "If I only knew back then what I know now." What is it that I know now that I wish I had known back then? Honestly, it's what I'm trying to write in the pages of this book. Yes, this book is entitled "Rite of Passage," but it's about so much more. For years as a husband, father, businessman, deacon, choir member, quartet singer, and member of several community groups, I found I was running wide open. I never seemed to have enough time to do anything well. I was trying to do it all. Here's the problem with the way I was living: *I was missing it!*

In Chapter 3 I spent quite a bit of time sharing about the role of the church in helping families raise Christ-centered adults. We looked at many passages of Scripture and by now we should all realize that the responsibility of raising children falls to the parents, principally the fathers. Certainly, you can go back and review those passages found in Genesis 18:19, Deuteronomy 6:1-7, Psalm 78 and Ephesians 6:4 any time you would like. The point is clear: *fathers are to be leading the way in discipling in our homes.* The truth is that I wasn't leading in my home even 10 years ago. I hate to admit it, but it is the truth. I was succeeding in everything except in being the spiritual leader in my home. What became crystal clear to me through several incidents and God-ordained experiences was the fact I needed to change or I would lose my family. Am I saying my wife was going to walk out on me and take the kids? Not necessarily, but I am saying I was in danger of raising children that would potentially never truly see a genuine, sincere faith in Jesus Christ. I was leaving this teaching to others because I was too busy to oversee it. I had been climbing the proverbial ladder of success and when I reached the top, I found that the ladder was leaning against the wrong wall.

Why am I taking the time to tell you all of this? Because I want you to know and understand that I am where I am today, in pursuit of building a Christ-directed life, by the grace and mercy of God. The whole idea of *Rite of Passage* is something that God has revealed to me gradually over the years and it has been a process for me. I didn't just get here overnight. What I am providing in the pages of this book is a culmination of the last ten years of my life. Indeed, I have learned the hard way what the Bible teaches about leading in my home, and I'm still learning.

As I think back, I realize I wasn't making disciples of my children because I didn't understand what was involved. I thought if I got my family to church each Sunday and I served on a few committees and tithed, I had my bases covered. Yet, I knew there was more. But, what was it? Did I need to serve more or be more involved at the church or give more money? What was this nagging in my soul? Finally, I attended a conference where I was challenged as a man. I had never been challenged like this before in the spiritual realm. I had been challenged as an athlete, at the office and even in the studio recording a CD with the quartet, but never like this. The Scriptures opened my eyes to what I knew intuitively, but couldn't quite grasp: *I must truly become a disciple of Christ to make disciples.* I must lead in my home by dying to myself. I realized for the first time in my life that it was my job to disciple my children, not that of my wife, not the church, or anyone else. This was a life-changing experience for me that sent me on a journey that has since led me to some amazing places.

I can often be an open book about my life. Some may say that I'm too open. I guess that's probably true, but I sincerely believe it's important that you know where I'm coming from, particularly if you are a dad reading this book. Please hear my heart! I was a successful business man, had a good marriage and wonderful children. I had also been to the top of what most laymen would consider the pinnacle of Christian service. Yet, I wouldn't trade anything for the way my wife and children look at me now. Something amazing happened in my life over a period of about nine months of soul-searching, fasting and prayer. The Lord transformed my thoughts, simplified my focus and challenged me to do what he created me to do. He had given me a passion for truly becoming a committed, dedicated disciple of Christ. My desires changed dramatically. God turned my heart toward my home and discipling my children.

CHANGED PERSPECTIVES

I knew that I was a Christian; however, there was a depth of commitment to Jesus Christ that I had never known before. I was living on the periphery of deep commitment. Yes, I was a believer and follower of Christ, but I thought, let's not get crazy. We don't want to go too deep with all of this, right? Jesus calls us to a radical lifestyle. He calls us to hunger and thirst for righteousness. He calls us to holiness and purity. That means I don't watch anything questionable on TV and I don't listen to ungodly music on the radio. Do you know what's funny? I didn't use to think I did either of those things, but I did. I was watching TV shows filled with sexual innuendo and bathroom humor, and I never thought anything about it. As I began to study the Bible, God revealed these things to me very clearly. I was listening to the same music everyone else was, yet it was filled with impure lyrics. Finally, my mind was opened to the truth of Scripture, such as Ephesians 5:3-4 (NIV):

> But among you there must not be even a hint of sexual immorality, or of any kind of impurity, or of greed, because these are improper for God's holy people. Nor should there be obscenity, foolish talk or coarse joking, which are out of place, but rather thanksgiving.

Not even a hint of sexual immorality. No obscenity. Do you know what that means? This Scripture teaches as a follower of Christ, I am not to watch, listen or read anything that has any sexual immorality or obscenity. No foolish talk or coarse joking. No off-color emails or jokes (spread through social websites or otherwise) are acceptable. As I continued to read and study Scripture, as I never had before, I was challenged by passages I had heard all of my life, but now saw differently. For instance, Romans 12:1-2:

> I appeal to you therefore, brothers, by the mercies of God, to present your bodies as a living sacrifice, holy and acceptable to God, which is your spiritual worship. Do not be conformed to this world, but be transformed by the renewal of your mind, that by testing you may discern what is the will of God, what is good and acceptable and perfect.

I discovered I was to be a walking dead man. That's what it means to be a living sacrifice. I learned I am to be holy. Yes, as believers we are called to be holy, but, I had excused away this whole idea by saying, "No one is perfect." So, I didn't even attempt to live a holy and righteous life. Don't get me wrong. I was good, as compared to the worst "Christians" I knew; but being holy and righteous, only Jesus could embody those qualities. I had been deceived. So, many things changed in my home. This is not to say we had a home filled with overtly sinful things. We didn't. As a family, we decided to do our very best to live a sacrificial life before the Lord. Therefore, TV shows, music and movie preferences changed. I remember distinctly getting emails that would have been considered coarse joking, that I deleted and didn't forward. Coincidentally, I no longer get those kinds of emails. I suppose those who were sending them saw something different in me, or so I hope.

I slowly began to untangle myself from the world and secular worldviews that had been filling my brain since childhood. I became a student of the Bible. I sincerely began studying the Scriptures. I replaced so much wasted time watching TV and surfing the internet with Scripture reading and Scripture memory. It is true that you will never be any better in public than what you are in private. I had to sacrifice sleep in order to get up early, get into the Word and meet with Jesus. I realized that for years I desired sleep more than I desired being with the Lord. Over time, my walk with the Lord became so much sweeter and more relaxed. It's difficult to describe in words, but I hope what I have shared helps you to understand what God was doing in my life.

MAKING DISCIPLES

So, what had happened to me? I had become a true disciple of Christ. Not just a passive believer, but sincerely an active follower and eager student of Christ. I genuinely wanted to be like Christ, not just identify with him, but to be like him. As the transformation of my mind continued, I saw my children changing as well. They saw a different Daddy. My home was becoming a disciple-making center instead of a place where I ran to get away from the world. When I turned the knob on the door to my house at the end of the day, I had a new attitude. I no longer thought, "Great, I can have some me time, and rest up for another day." No, as I turned the knob to the door of my home each evening, I thought, "Behind that door is where I must succeed first."

I have learned that succeeding at home requires perseverance, not perfection. Dads, we will not be flawless. But we can learn how to reserve energy so that we don't come home from work so emotionally exhausted that we have nothing left for our wives and children. We can choose not to bend to selfishness, but instead to make up our minds to invest in the next generation. I have finally learned that I need to save some energy for home. My motto is now: *Save Some for Home.*

Jesus said, "Go and make disciples of all nations" (Matt. 28:19). He also said, "Be my witnesses in Jerusalem, and in all Judea and Samaria, and to the ends of the earth" (Acts 1:8). I discovered that my Jerusalem, which is my local community, must begin in my home. In Scripture this is a mandate for church leaders. Paul clearly told Timothy in 1 Timothy 3:4-5:

> *He must manage his own household well, with all dignity keeping his children submissive, for if someone does not know how to manage his own household, how will he care for God's church?*

This passage is not just for elders or pastors, it's for all men. He must manage his own household well. He must do so with dignity and his children must be submissive. That means they are respectful among other things.

The Hebraic form of teaching was led by the fathers in the home. They had charge over the spiritual discipleship of the children. Today, many have left this to the women or to the church, because many men think this is "beneath them" or even silly. We would rather spend our time in other more manly pursuits. We just say that we don't have time. Yet, if you are still taking the *Sola Scriptura* challenge, from Chapter 1, we understand the Bible says it is the father's responsibility to manage his own household. I certainly count on my wife, Pam, to help, but the weight and responsibility falls on my shoulders, not hers. Yet, for too many years she managed our household, because I wasn't getting the job done. I'm grateful for a wife who stepped up when I had stepped out. I understand now and I hope you do as well, that in order to make disciples, one must be a disciple.

We must ask ourselves some very sobering questions. Are you a disciple of Jesus Christ or are you living on the outskirts of Christianity? Have you surrendered your all to Jesus, or just that which comes easy? Does he own all of you—your life, your dreams, your aspirations and your heart? Where is your treasure? You will find your treasure where you find your heart. What is it that you can't get enough of? That is probably your god. How can we raise Christ-centered children if we aren't Christ-centered, ourselves? Luke tells us, "A disciple is not above his teacher, but everyone when he is fully trained will be like his teacher." What are we teaching our children?

We must change the mindset that raising children is something we complete when they are 18 or 21. Raising children is a lifelong endeavor. Not only that, it should be a multi-generational endeavor. Look beyond your lifetime. Can you see in your mind's eye into the future and visualize your great-grandchildren? What will they say about you? What do you want them to say about you? In the Old Testament the Lord allowed his name to be spoken of as the "God of Abraham, Isaac and Jacob." That's multi-generational! I want my grandchildren and great-grandchildren to look back and say, "He was a man of God that passed his faith in Christ on to us." ROP is about passing the baton of our faith in Jesus Christ to the next generation, so they will pass it to the next generation. ROP is a conduit through which our children pass from their childhood to adulthood with an ownership of faith in God. We must begin making disciples in our homes, our Jerusalem, as we go from there to the uttermost parts of the earth. If we get it right everywhere else, but get it wrong at home, we have failed.

MAKING DISCIPLES TAKES TIME

I love to garden. I've been gardening for years and it is very therapeutic for me, not to mention that it saves a lot of money on the grocery bill. A few years ago, my daughter Clara and I were planting the garden. It's a process that usually takes one day each spring. We lined off the garden by making rows in the soil and then we planted our crop. Usually, we plant mostly green beans, cucumbers, cantaloupes, tomatoes and corn. Clara worked so hard helping me. When we were finished that evening, she was so excited! My five-year-old daughter then exclaimed, "Daddy, I can't wait till tomorrow morning to go pick all the beans and corn!" Clara didn't understand. She thought the process of the seed turning to plant, turning to blooms, turning to fruit happened overnight. I wish it did, but as we all know, it doesn't.

Gardening takes time and so does making disciples. It took Jesus three years to teach, train and equip his followers. Yet, they still struggled mightily. Peter comes to mind immediately. After three years of intense time with him, Peter denied even knowing Jesus three times. He even called down curses upon himself. Jesus never gave up on Peter. Peter was slow to learn, just like so many of us. If anyone could attest to the fact that making disciples is a long and hard process, it would be Jesus.

Raising a family is much like riding a roller coaster. There will be many ups and downs. We get to choose our attitude and how we will respond to those ups and downs. Still, it is easy to get impatient and tired of the tedious work. ROP is not guaranteed to make this process any less tedious. It is not some sort of 8-week program that is going to magically change your life or that of your child. ROP is a process, like gardening that begins when the children are no more than a seed and takes much time to plant, weed, water, fertilize and pray through the droughts and storms of life. One can also see ROP as a way of living or a lifestyle that is like driving a car on a mountain road. We must not take our hands off the steering wheel for long or we will wreck, guaranteed!

168 Hours

Understanding that making disciples takes time, let's look at how we spend our time and see what kind of time we have available to us in order to do so. We all know there are 168 hours in a week. None of us get any more or any less time. It doesn't matter if one is rich or poor, we all get the same amount of time. There are 60 minutes in an hour, 24 hours in a day, 7 days in a week and that equates to 168 hours per week for each of us.

Through the years I've conducted an unscientific poll that I believe is fairly accurate in regards to how we spend our time. I've discovered the average person sleeps somewhere around 8 hours per night (again, these are averages). Therefore, the average person sleeps around 56 hours per week. We work around 60 hours per week. You may say, "I don't work that much!" Actually, that 60-hour number includes the following: getting ready for work (shower/make-up, etc), driving to work, actually working, and driving home from work. So, on average we spend around 116 of our 168 hours, almost 70% of our time, per week just sleeping and doing things related to work. That leaves 58 hours. Over the years I have found most of us spend about 4 hours per day, or about 28 hours per week, doing things like: preparing and eating meals, cleaning up from meals, paying bills, doing laundry, cleaning the house, doing yard work and the like. These are things that we must do in order to live. These are the things we have little choice in whether we do them or not. What does that leave us? It leaves about 24 hours per week or just a little over 3 hours per day of what could be considered *disposable time*.

Disposable time is just that. It is time that is disposable to us. Let's assume we have a scenario where there are children still in the home and both parents work. So, we have three hours per day that we can use any way we wish. Now when do we normally get this time? Think it through. In a normal work week, the average person is up in the morning getting ready for work or school or the activities of that day. We head off to school and work and then get home or off work around 5 or 6 pm. Many families are dual-income families, where the mother and father both work. Most families have children in school. In most instances families are going to find their disposable time after dinner is finished around 6:30 pm. If that is the case (I know I'm making quite a few assumptions) we have approximately three hours at our disposal. This time will most likely be available between 6:30 pm and 9:30 pm, give or take a little. Most families with smaller children have them in the bed by 9:30 pm. (Again, this is a generalization.) If the children are older, they are most likely in their rooms by then, most likely on the computer, doing homework or watching TV.

I've not even mentioned the weekend at this point. Saturdays mean different things to different people. Some work, while others play, do yard work, play golf, shop, etc. Needless to say, in most homes, little spiritual training takes place on Saturdays. We know there are always things to get done. Some obsess so much with keeping the house or car clean that they don't spend time with their family. Some "play" all weekend. Weekends are "fun time" for the family. There is a balance to be found here. Certainly, I'm assuming we are all in church on Sunday. But I'm principally focusing on the work week.

The elaborate scenario I've presented should poignantly emphasize that what you and I do at night is crucial in the *disciple-making* venture that is ours. Remember that approximately 24 hours per week is disposable. What does this mean? It means we don't have much time to get the job done of raising a Christ-centered family. If we are going to deliver to our children a faith in Christ that is rock solid, we must guard our time like a precious treasure and use it wisely. But do we?

THE AMERICAN DREAM

Most families in America, Christian or not, seek the American Dream. I'm not going to try to define this phenomenon, because it means different things to different people. However, most people see it as the pursuit of happiness and getting all the gusto out of life one can. So, we pack our schedules with all the activities we can afford in pursuit of happiness and the American Dream. Many American families are seldom home at night during the week. They are constantly on the move. There are after-school activities, ball practices, extra-curricular classes, dance lessons, music lessons, tutoring, etc. The list can go on and on.

If you ask one of these family members how they are doing they will say, "I'm tired." Sure they are tired. They are running from pillar to post and are utterly exhausted. Why? Because it is exhausting to pursue the American Dream. Is there anything inherently wrong with this pursuit and all of these activities? We all want our children to be well-rounded. But, we must ask ourselves this question: *When are we supposed to disciple the children?* When do we become students of the Word of God? When do we, ourselves, have time to become disciples so that we can in turn make disciples, if we are running around all over the place, all the time? That's precisely the problem. If we are never together for more than a few minutes here and there, we can't and we won't make disciples.

Is our American Dream that important? Do our children have to have it all? What are we saying to our children? How are they establishing their identity? Is it in *what they do* (their activities) or *who* they are? Often I hear parents describe children in this way. They will say, "I know her. She's a cheerleader at the middle school." Or perhaps this way: "He's the point guard on the basketball team at the high school." They are known as the cheerleader, the basketball player, the dancer, the piano player, the smart kid, etc. We establish in the minds of our children, unknowingly, that they must be identified by whatever they participate in to be somebody. It is easy to see why we do so. It's because of this pursuit of happiness and the fact that we equate happiness and our identity with *going* and *doing* and getting all we can out of life.

Many have become so enamored by the idea of the American Dream that they equate their success with it. These false, pagan ideals bombard us at every turn. They are in the grocery store check-out line. Those skinny beauties on magazine covers that say, "You can have it all if you look like me." Commercials and billboards flash before our eyes flaunting the "good life." They say things like: drink this, buy this, or have this and you'll be happy. Americans today buy lottery tickets by the millions just hoping and praying they can hit the jackpot and get rich; then all their dreams will come true. One dream embodies all those dreams—the American Dream. But we Christians are wiser than those who pursue such frivolity, aren't we? We can have our cake and eat it too! We can have it all (the big house, nice cars, vacations, new clothes, nice TVs, the latest gadgets) and still raise our children right, can't we? As long as they are well-educated, accomplished and well-liked, then all is well or is it?

SPORTS AND ACADEMICS

Many families in America are very active in sports. Obviously sports are very important to us in our nation, because we value our top athletes so much that we pay them exorbitant and excessively high salaries as professionals. I was very involved in sports as a child and I really enjoyed basketball in particular. I am 6'6" tall so basketball was a sensible choice. But, I really regret the amount of time I wasted *just* playing basketball. I was out of balance. I was spending inordinate amounts of time playing basketball in comparison to other endeavors in my life.

I often see the same thing happening in many homes. The schedule for the home is dictated by the season of year. I am not talking about winter, spring, summer or fall; I'm talking about the *sports season*. We have to look on the refrigerator at the schedule to see if we can do anything. Many families are involved in weekend sports with teams that travel many weekends throughout the year. Many dads have come to me and said, "Pastor Kevin, you won't be seeing us much for the next several months because my son has travel ball, you know. But we'll see you soon." It is interesting to notice how many of these dads take such an interest in their children's success on a ball field or court.

I've heard the stories, and you have too, where the wife goes to the back door of the home and yells out to her husband and son to come in for dinner. For example, they have been practicing pitching a baseball. The dad yells back, "Be there in a minute! He's almost got his curve ball breaking over the plate perfectly!" Is there anything wrong with this scenario? Absolutely not. It's wonderful to have a father who is engaged in his son's or daughter's life. But, what if this scene takes place most nights of the week? This backyard practice doesn't include the practicing after school or the games. It is in addition to the team practices and games. Once we add up all the time and energy, there is a huge investment here. Have you heard of this scenario happening before? A wife yells up the stairs to her husband and son to come to dinner and the husband yells back, "Be down in a minute! We are almost finished memorizing this passage of Scripture!" Ever heard of that happening? Maybe it has, but probably not nearly as often as the first scenario.

We are sports obsessed in this nation. It is amazing how much we put a premium on those who are good at sports. I'm not against sports. I love sports. I love playing sports of all kinds and attending games. I played in high school and in college. All of my coaches made high demands of me. Any coach or instructor is going to push athletes to get the most out of them. This is expected. Parents often tell me about their children and their commitments to their coaches and teams. In the same breath they tell me because of the upcoming game they can't keep their commitment to the church. Seems like a double standard.

Sports activities are not the only obsessions we have turned into gods in many of our homes. As I mentioned I believe many are worshiping the god called *academic success*. This god is on display in all circles of academia, including public, private, charter, Christian or schools within the home. Parents love speaking about how well their children are doing in school. There is certainly nothing wrong with academic success. I graduated at the top of my class in high school and in college. But, we must remember the words of the Apostle John when he said, "I have no greater joy than to hear that my children are walking in the truth" (3 John 4). Can we say that? Does our desire for academic or athletic success for our children eclipse this standard written by John? God does not have a room in heaven for our children's diplomas and trophies. I can hear the words of the 12-year-old Jesus again. Can you hear them? He said he had to be about his Father's business. What about our children? What or whose business are they about?

We push our children academically and athletically. We want them to be the best they can possibly be in these areas. But what about spiritually—do we push them spiritually? Somehow, we have tied our children's success, and in many cases, their identity, to how well they perform on the field, dance floor, court or classroom. We push them to get scholarships and get high grades in school. Then what? They graduate with a degree and get a job and start making money. Does that bring happiness and fulfillment? Jesus said we should seek the kingdom of God first and then everything else we need will be added to us (see Matt. 6:33). We might say we believe this for our children and we may even tell them that, but what do our actions show? Many seem to be seeking first the kingdom of education and sports. Some families make their kids do homework during church services of all things. Homework should be done, but there is a time for it. Shouldn't God come first, even above homework? Some miss church because they have to study for the big test the next day or practice for the big game later in the week. Why should we be dismayed or astounded when they go to college and have no desire to go to church? Our actions have spoken loudly to our children while growing up. Now they are placing other things before God, just like we did.

We must count the cost. We really cannot have it all. We may have to choose. Do we want our children to make straight-A's or take some time to learn the Word of God and make B's? Would we be willing for our children not to be on the travel team, even though they may be good enough, so they can be in church and have time to be at home for more spiritual training? There is a cost and a huge price to be paid if you desire to have a ROP home. It is so easy to get tangled up in living vicariously through the successes of our children, especially if they can do things we were unable to do as a child. It is not an all or nothing proposition. We must find a balance for sure. But, choose wisely and remember, whatever it is that we make our children crave is what they will desire for the rest of their lives. If we were to ask our children about their goals in life, what would be their response? What would their answers reveal? What do they crave? What kind of legacy are we passing down to our children? Is it the American Dream, or a Christ-honoring life? Is a little Jesus here and a little Jesus there good enough?

THE MEDICINE DROPPER APPROACH

If you have been a parent long, you know from time to time you will have sick children on your hands. If they are small enough, you will most likely end up using a little medicine dropper to give them medicine. A medicine dropper is that small tube with the rubber end that you stick down into the medicine bottle and squeeze, pulling up the medicine into the dropper. It usually holds about one teaspoon of medicine. Ultimately, you place the dropper into the mouth of the child and release the medicine, praying it will make them well soon.

I believe we have this same approach with our children concerning their spirituality. We seem to be using a medicine dropper of Jesus and praying that a little dab will do. If our kids are young, we may have a prayer with them at bedtime or perhaps a prayer before the meal, but that's about the extent of our spiritual time. As we discussed, many families seldom even eat at home because they are on the move from practice to practice, game to game and lesson to lesson, almost every night of the week. Our minivans and cars have become our dinner tables. Time is of the essence.

Still, we say that our children are at church on Sundays and Wednesdays. But that is just not enough. It is like saying an occasional rain shower or just a little bit of sun will make a bountiful and fruitful garden. It won't. A garden needs enormous amounts of sun, water and fertilizer to grow. It is wonderful that we take our children to church. However, as we learned in Chapter 3, the church house was never intended to be the place where the real discipling is accomplished. That job must be done in the home by the parents. For most, we have become convinced that the medicine dropper approach will work. I thought this for a long time. But, we live in a culture today that is making our children very sick, not literally, but sin-sick. They are inundated with worldviews and philosophies that are so pagan and anti-God that it is staggering to the mind. In many schools children are taught from the first grade that their ancestors are monkeys. They are fed a steady diet of pop culture through TV, music, video games and every other form of media. Even in a controlled atmosphere, they are contaminated every day by a mixed up world. So, a medicine dropper of Jesus and discipleship simply won't work! They need more, much more. They need Jesus and the Word of God to be flowing through them like an IV-drip.

If you have ever been around a hospital, you have seen plenty of IV bags hanging from little metal stands on rollers. If the patient is sick enough, he must take that IV bag of medicine everywhere he goes. If he takes a walk down the hall, the IV goes too. The patient must receive a constant flow of his or her medicine and when the IV bag runs out, the monitor on the rolling stand signals an alarm. It beeps and beeps until the nurse comes and replaces the used bag with a new, full bag of medicine. Likewise, we must be constantly pumping Christ's teachings and the Bible into our young people from a very early age to counteract the influences and worldviews of evolutionary thinking and secular humanism going into them. As good as most of our schools are in America, these schools and their teachers cannot and will not teach our children about Jesus Christ. As good as our coaches and instructors may be it is not their responsibility to teach our children the Bible and the principles of Scripture.

What is the worldview or way of thinking of so many of our children? It is whatever is consistently and regularly poured into their lives. More succinctly, the worldview of your children's teachers, coaches, instructors, and tutors will likely become a large part of their worldview (good or bad). They will adopt the worldview of the music they listen to, TV shows and movies they watch. The way their friends think and what they see on social websites could easily become their worldview. It is impossible to over-compensate and counter-balance this secular mindset with the medicine dropper approach of teaching the Scriptures and giving them Jesus.

WHAT ARE WE POURING INTO THEIR LIVES?

Let's envision our children as empty vessels or cups to be filled. Each and every day they are being filled by what they are taught through what they see and hear. The average American child will spend most of the day at school, where they can't hear about the Lord and will learn from a secular point of view. It doesn't mean the school is bad or the teachers are bad, but the principles of Scripture can't be taught in our public schools. This can only be done in private, Christian or home schools. After school, they will come home and most often spend time watching TV, playing video games, texting, chatting or tweeting friends. Many will then make the nightly trek to a myriad of other activities. Finally, at some point, we may grab a few minutes with our children. What should we do? We need to have meaningful conversations about their day to discover what they are learning and the mindset and framework in which they are learning it. To use a term from the military, we need to bring in our soldiers and *debrief* them about the activities of the day and then help them understand what they have heard and seen through the framework and grid of Scripture. This takes time. It takes a lot of time. How, then, do we raise children in a framework that will one day graduate them to spiritual adulthood?

It all comes down to how we utilize the time and what we pour into our children's cups. We have no choice but to make time to talk to them and to teach them God's truth. It is about making the wisest use of the time. We all get the same 168 hours per week. We must redeem the time. We must take back our nights and gain control of our schedules. Paul said to the church at Ephesus in Ephesians 5:15-16, "Look carefully then how you walk, not as unwise but as wise, making the best use of the time, because the days are evil." We are going to have to *simplify* our lives and even *downsize*, in many cases, to make the best use of the time. What does that mean? We have to slow down and re-prioritize. If we want to raise Christ-centered children, we must invest time in them. You may have heard this said before, but children spell love: T-I-M-E. If we really love our kids, the way they need to be loved, we will spend time with them and I'm not just talking about quality time. I'm talking about quality and quantity time. That time must be used to model Christian principles and beliefs that will be indelibly branded into our children forever, so that future generations will know God as well.

MAKING THE INVESTMENT

We all know raising children is hard! It is a difficult, time consuming, often thankless job. Yet, the Bible teaches that children are a heritage from the Lord. They are indeed a reward from him. Our life is a race and we must realize the investment that must be made if we are going to pass to our children the baton of faith in Jesus Christ. Remember the words of Deuteronomy 6:5-7.

> *You shall love the LORD your God with all your heart and with all your soul and with all your might. And these words that I command you today shall be on your heart. You shall teach them diligently to your children, and shall talk of them when you sit in your house, and when you walk by the way, and when you lie down, and when you rise.*

We are commanded to teach our children how to love the Lord with all of their heart, soul and might. The words of the Lord are to be on our hearts. We are to diligently teach them to our children. Think about the word "diligently." What do we do "diligently" in our lives? What motivates us to work hard? As parents, with the father leading, we are to teach our children the commands of God when we sit, walk, lie down and rise up. The Lord, through Moses, tells us we must take time to *diligently* teach our children.

The Scripture tells us we must be talking about the Lord consistently and constantly to our children. We do this when we are sitting together and talking about the Lord and his commands. Watching TV or a movie together doesn't qualify. That's not teaching time. That's entertainment time. There must be times where the Scriptures are read and discussed in our homes and we can slow down and focus. For so many, if we do any sort of family devotions, we do so with great haste. This process of teaching is more than just sitting through a devotion or Bible lesson time. The Scripture teaches we are to talk about the commands of the Lord all the time. We do so when we are making dinner together and thanking the Lord for the food. When we are folding clothes, we should be praising the Lord for clothing and for shelter. We do this at bedtime when we talk and share with the children. Many say that the 15-20 minutes before your children go to sleep is when they are most open and willing to talk. Don't rush by those bedtime conversations. Much listening, learning and teaching can take place right before all is quiet in the house. Even at breakfast, when we rise up, we should be teaching. We should be teaching all the time.

Many families struggle with finding time to study the Bible together. I often tell people they must schedule time with the Lord. We write on our calendars what is important such as doctor appointments, dentist appointments, our kids' games, recitals, etc. If necessary, do the same with devotion times. Schedule it! You may begin with only one or two nights per week. Just start. Make it happen.

As you can see, it takes a great deal of this precious commodity called time to train and teach our children. It certainly takes more than a few minutes here and a couple of minutes there each day. We must give our children large doses of biblical teaching and give it very often. If we don't teach them in this manner, watch what happens when young adults go off to college their freshman year and return home at Thanksgiving. You will hear them espouse, "I don't believe that way anymore, Dad." Often, when a young adult gets to college their faith is challenged. In fact, everything they believe about Christianity is challenged, including the authority of the Bible as God's Word. Often their faith crumbles and they begin to view Christianity as only one of many choices on the buffet line of religions the world and Satan offers. Therefore, it is true, in just weeks the children we raised and knew so well come home to us and seem like strangers.

I hear many stories like this. People tell me they can't understand how their child could have changed so much in just 2 ½ months in college. They say, "We taught them for 18 years about the Lord and in just a few weeks all of that has unraveled." At this point parents must spend a lot of time on their knees asking God to intervene in their young adult's life. It is sobering to think about, but maybe their independence and higher education just helped along the process that had been occurring, almost imperceptibly under our noses, for several years. What we see didn't just happen. It had already occurred years ago and was simply buried. Perhaps college or independence just brought to the surface the fact that he or she wasn't truly a believer.

What many parents miss is that their children may have already checked out spiritually. They may continue to sit in our pews or padded chairs each week, but somewhere along the way they decided to just go through the motions. It reminds me of the words of Jesus when he said, "These people honor me with their lips, but their hearts are far from me" (Mark 7:6). So they come to church with us and they are good kids, participating in church functions and activities; however if someone were to probe deeper, they would find little spiritual depth beyond a salvation experience and baptism. The concept of ROP helps us to go beyond the surface of a young person's spirituality. It causes the parents and child to go deeper and see what is at the root of a young person's Christian life and experience. ROP itself is a barometer that helps us to measure if there has been a genuine conversion and if so, whether or not enough time is being invested in that young person's life to actually grow them in Christ.

FEEDING THE GOOD DOG OR THE BAD DOG

We all have appetites. As Christians we have two natures or appetites. One appetite is for the things of God or the Spirit, while the other is for sinful things or the flesh. These appetites are at battle within our minds and the minds of our children. They are like two dogs fighting against one another. Whatever appetite or dog we feed becomes the strongest. If we feed the sinful dog things like questionable movies, TV shows, music and video games, that dog, the flesh, will grow and dominate the other. If we feed the spiritual dog things like Bible teaching, Scripture memory, wholesome TV, movies and music, good books, adult interaction and conversation, etc. the spirit will grow.

Sometimes we feed the fleshly appetites in our children unknowingly. We can dress our daughters in cute revealing outfits when they are young and feed the appetite of immodesty in our teen girls. A short skirt on an 8-year-old might look cute, but on a 16-year-old it sends much different signals. So, why put it on the 8-year-old in the first place? We can encourage and allow violent video games for our boys to play and feed the appetite of rage and violence that leads to lawlessness. We can tell the 4th graders that are "in love" that it is OK to sit holding hands together. But, those 4th graders grow up to get their license and drive cars and the hand holding that has been allowed for years steadily grows to feed the lust of promiscuous relationships during the teen years. In the book *Family Driven Faith*, Dr. Voddie Baucham describes the problem. Writes Baucham (Baucham, 21):

Modern American dating is no more than glorified divorce practice. Young people are learning how to give themselves away in exclusive, romantic, highly committed (at times sexual) relationships, only to break up and do it all over again. God never intended for his kids to live like this. And instead of stepping in and doing something, many Christian parents, simply view these types of relationships as a normal and necessary part of growing up. Unless your child is wiser than Solomon, stronger than Samson, and more godly than David (all of whom sinned sexually), they are susceptible to sexual sin, and these premature relationships serve as open invitations.

Things that seem harmless for children when they are young will most often grow into big, hungry dogs in older years. We must understand that God knows exactly who our child's husband or wife is going to be. If he is all-knowing, and he is, then we must trust that he will orchestrate the circumstances to bring them together. We, nor our children, need to do this for God. He is more than capable. Being involved in exclusive relationships before you are ready to be married is like going shopping without any money. Doing so will leave you frustrated, or you will take something that doesn't belong to you. We must pray for God's discernment that we do not feed the wrong dog in our children concerning relationships with the opposite sex. *Whatever we allow in moderation, they will take to excess.*

Feeding the good in our children may mean cutting back in some areas that aren't necessarily bad. We may have to come to the point that we are willing to sacrifice the *good* so that we may have the *best* for our children. This may require us to have some difficult conversations with our children. For instance, it may mean explaining that the goal of raising them to be a disciple of Christ will require cutting back on extra-curricular activities. Believe me, this is where it gets hard. If you have raised your child on a steady diet of activities, sports, hobbies, lessons, etc. outside the home, and you begin curtailing those activities, they will most likely balk. But if we are going to train young people to be mature, Christ-following adults, we will have to do the hard things.

GATEKEEPERS

As parents, principally the fathers, we are given the responsibility of being the gate keeper of our homes. That means we must monitor everything that comes into our family and our home. Everything should pass through the filter of God's Word before it is allowed past the gate. Fathers ultimately, are completely accountable to God for what and whom we allow into our homes via the door, TV, computer, phones, etc. The hard part about this is technology is increasing at such a rapid pace that it is very hard to keep up, particularly if your young children have computers and cell phones at their disposal, 24-7. We will protect our children from robbers and thieves, but Satan who has come to steal, kill and destroy is more subtle than any burglar. He comes in the back door of our lives, not the front. He makes no grand entrances or introductions. He is an unwelcome guest that enters our home as quickly as a fly through an open door. Are we watching for him or have we been lulled to sleep?

As parents, we must be better students of the Word of God than even our parents. The culture is much tougher to navigate than it was in their day. We must become savvy students of Scripture and be able to teach Christian apologetics to our children. We must give answers for the difficult and troubling questions of life. We can no longer think we can spend a few spare minutes a day with our children, drop them off at youth group at church and get the job done of raising a Christ-centered young adult. How could we ever think a couple of hours a week at youth group and a prayer over a meal here and there would ever be enough to raise grounded, solid believers in Christ? Christianity is only one generation from extinction. Each generation lives with that fact.

So, we must make time to teach our children the ways of the Lord and we must understand that if we don't, we *will* lose this generation.

TIME AT HOME

Today, time at home for most families is hard to find. Even if you are home several nights per week as a family, it is easy to waste that time as well. Just because the family is all gathered together doesn't mean that we are really *together*. Many families are living separate lives under the same roof. For example, the dad is in one room watching sports on TV, the kids are in their rooms on the computer or cell phone and the mom may be surfing the web or catching up with friends on a social website in yet another room. Everyone is home, but separate. So many homes operate in this manner. They co-exist in the same house, but have little time invested in one another. There is a price to be paid to get everyone's schedules together and place a priority on conversation, discussion and the study of the Word of God.

If you make the decision to pay that price and truly come together as a family, then you may wonder where to begin. My answer is short and simple: you begin by coming together physically in the same room. This can be in the den, kitchen or someone's bedroom. We often have our devotion time around the dinner table. We push the dishes to the center and pull out our Bibles and prepare for family devotions. My wife and I use the Word of God extensively to teach and train in our home. Certainly there are many devotion books on the market and there are many ways of going about this process. However, I've found just following the guidance of Scripture itself and to study it "to show thyself approved" is the most effective way that works for our family. We have Study Bibles and often, we like to cross reference passages. We study the Bible mostly by individual books. We just finished studying 2 Timothy. We read the entire book every day for one week. It's only four chapters and even a slow reader can do so in about 15 minutes.

Once we get a good grasp of the overall tone of the book, we begin to break it down, verse by verse. This is when we begin doing a lot of cross referencing using the little, small letters in the text and central margins to help us better learn and understand the passages. I do have commentaries and concordances galore and these can prove to be useful. But the Holy Spirit teaches and leads us and other opinions and interpretations are secondary.

Must we be dogmatic and spend every night in a two-hour long devotion? No, there is no need to be legalistic. The time you spend will depend on the age and maturity of the children in your home. Of course, as has been said, we should spend large amounts of time in the Word of God if we love the Lord. It should be a pleasure to do so. Truthfully, this is when we can begin to ascertain the spiritual depth of our children. What do they say when you call throughout the house: "Time for devotion!" Do they cringe and whine, complaining incessantly? Are they learning the Word? Do they spend time in the Word on their own? What is their appetite for Bible study? We can tell during these devotion times in our homes about the spiritual temperature of our families. Are we hot, cold or lukewarm? Think with me about what a typical week looks like in your home. Think about last week for instance or the week before. What did you do each night of the past two weeks? How did you spend your time with your family? What may need to change? What price are you willing to pay to redeem the time in your home?

A LEGACY

The ROP approach embodies leaving a legacy for our children. One of the things I ask participants each year in our church's ROP is to learn about their family on both their father's and mother's side of the family. There is much to be learned from digging into our family history. Think of the Scriptures. There are many lists of names and lineages in the Bible. We see in the book of Matthew the ancestry of Jesus from both Mary and Joseph. We are all given a family legacy at birth. We didn't ask for it, pay for it, earn it or even desire it, yet it was given to us simply because we were born. We give our children, grandchildren and great-grandchildren a legacy as well. What will we give them? What will they remember about us and how we spent our lives? Are we spending our lives pursuing the material things of this earth as little more than "wage slaves" or are we spending our lives serving the Master of the universe? After all, Jesus said we should store up our treasures in heaven where moths and rust won't destroy or thieves won't break in and steal. What kind of legacy are we leaving for our children? Are we pointing them to Jesus? Do they see us pursuing Christ or trinkets in an earthly treasure pile? Are we living for the praise and accolades of man or do we want to hear instead, "Well done, good and faithful servant?"

Solomon said, "A good man leaves an inheritance for his children's children ..." (Prov. 13:22a). An inheritance can be money, but it is also much more. Money means nothing when a loved one dies. When a father or mother passes away, we remember what they said to us and taught us. It really isn't about the money or it shouldn't be. Those memories or legacies left behind from their words and actions are those that we remember most. Those are priceless and something money can't buy. They are a legacy to be treasured.

Throughout Scripture we see legacies which were left by fathers to sons in particular. Abraham left a legacy of faith to his son Isaac and Isaac to his son Jacob. But, think about it. Do we see another set of father, son, and grandson listed together? If so, I have never found one. Why? I believe most fathers struggle with being the spiritual leader and model of the home. Fathers are often more concerned about making a name for themselves than being the spiritual head of the household. Remember, after Adam and Eve sinned in the Garden of Eden, they had to leave paradise and the ground was cursed because of sin. Adam, and therefore all men, have had to work by the sweat of their brow ever since. It's interesting that man defines himself most often by what he does for a living, while woman generally defines herself by her children and family. Both men and women are defined by the curses levied upon them; one the ground, the other childbearing. Men have always struggled with the tug-of-war between being the leader in the home versus being a success in the world, where his work is most often done and seen by the eyes of man.

In Scripture, this battle between work and home played out in the life of the Prophet Eli in 1 Samuel 2-4. Eli did a wonderful job in teaching and training Samuel, the young boy who was left with him by his parents, Elkanah and Hannah. This couple, in keeping a promise made to the Lord, brought Samuel to Eli to be raised before the Lord after Samuel was weaned. Eli taught Samuel how to hear from God and was his mentor. Eli did a superb job teaching and training Samuel, who would one day take over as Israel's prophet. Eli, in essence, was getting the job done at the office. But, Eli had two sons named Hophni and Phinehas. These boys were wicked in the eyes of the Lord. They were having inappropriate relations with women who served at the entrance to the Tent of Meeting (see 1 Sam. 2). Eli knew what his sons were doing and asked them to stop. However, they refused to listen and ultimately were killed by the Philistines. Eli, upon hearing the news about the death of his sons and the capture of the ark of God, fell backward off his chair, broke his neck and died. Unfortunately, Eli got it right at work, but missed it at home.

We see the same scenario throughout the Old Testament. If you read through the books of 1 Kings and 2 Kings and 1 and 2 Chronicles, you will not find a succession of three godly kings anywhere in the line of kings for the northern kingdom (Israel) or the southern kingdom (Judah). You will see a father like Solomon, who was given great wisdom, but was so busy growing his kingdom that he apparently forgot to properly train his sons. He told them in the book of Proverbs repeatedly to listen to his instruction and teaching. However, there is much training that must take place not by being told, but by watching the actions of men. Solomon's son, Rehoboam would not listen to the elders when he took over the kingdom from his father; instead he listened to his peers for advice (see 2 Chron. 10). Disaster fell upon Rehoboam and the kingdom was split because of his foolishness. What happened?

It seems Solomon was too busy expanding his kingdom and growing it instead of growing and training his son. 2 Chronicles 8:1-6 gives us details:

> *At the end of twenty years, in which Solomon had built the house of the LORD and his own house, Solomon rebuilt the cities that Hiram had given to him, and settled the people of Israel in them. And Solomon went to Hamath-zobah and took it. He built Tadmor in the wilderness and all the store cities that he built in Hamath. He also built Upper Beth-horon and Lower Beth-horon, fortified cities with walls, gates, and bars, and Baalath, and all the store cities that Solomon had and all the cities for his chariots and the cities for his horsemen, and whatever Solomon desired to build in Jerusalem, in Lebanon, and in all the land of his dominion.*

As a man, I understand how easy it is to get bogged down with work. I can easily be a workaholic. I have to constantly guard against this tendency. Even in writing this book, I have had to tell myself to stop and not sacrifice my children on the altar of my work. To be totally honest, it's really a pride issue. I suppose my hard work and diligence will show everyone that I'm a good pastor and they will think more highly of me. I can easily get my identity wrapped up in what I do. I believe Solomon did this too. Solomon's son did indeed take what he had allowed in moderation to excess. Solomon gave his sons all the rules in Proverbs, but where was the relationship? When did they spend time together? I have come to understand and firmly believe that rules without a relationship lead to rebellion.

There is an account in Scripture that encourages me greatly, however. It's an account of a young man named Ehud. He's tucked away in the Old Testament book of Judges (see Judg. 3:12-30). His swashbuckling exploits are amazingly daring and the story of his journey to kill the tyrant king, Eglon, keeps you on the edge of your seat. Ehud ultimately triumphs over the wicked king by stabbing him with a hand-made dagger. Israel is delivered by this young man's courage and valor. If you read this account and do a little studying, you will find Ehud is from the tribe of Benjamin. Those born in this tribe or family were all taught and trained to be left-handed. It didn't matter if they were right handed or not.

As is true today, and in the days of Ehud, most people are born right-handed (around 90%). Knowing this, the fathers in the tribe of Benjamin decided they would train their boys to be left-handed, so they would have an advantage in battle. In hand–to-hand combat these young men would begin the fight right-handed, then without notice they would suddenly switch the sword to the left hand, taking their baffled foe by complete surprise, thus slaying him. Ehud killed the wicked king using this left-handed method, taking him completely by surprise. You may ask, "What's the point?"

The men from the tribe of Benjamin, which literally means "son of the right hand," taught their sons to be different from everyone else. These men had a vision for their sons' success. They wanted to give them an advantage, but it would require much sacrifice, work and training. The fathers would tie their sons' right hands to their sides or behind their backs so they would learn to use their left hand. Does that sound cruel? Initially it does. But let's think of the outcome. These young boys were trained to be ambidextrous (see 1 Chron. 12:2). These fathers from the tribe of Benjamin had vision! Do you think the boys of this tribe felt strange and different? How did they feel compared to everyone else? Was it strange that they had to spend so much time being trained to be different? Perhaps so, but Scripture shows us these men of Benjamin were fighting machines. We must do the same in our day.

We are not talking about training soldiers for a literal battlefield where swords are wielded. We are talking about soldiers for Christ, who are willing to look different and act different from the world. We must raise warriors willing to *contend for the faith*, just as Paul told Timothy. So, in a sense, we are training our children to be "left-handed." Those who engage in this kind of parenting define success as intentionally training their children toward their transformation, rather than simply accepting the aging and survival of the child as satisfactory results. Parents, we must first be soldiers and warriors of the truth and of the Word of God ourselves before we can expect this from our children. How can we teach our children and expect them to be any better than we are? We must remember that reading and studying the Bible is our way of hearing from our maker, the creator of the universe. The Bible is God's love letter to us and it is also his instruction book for how we can make disciples for him. Through reading the Bible on a daily basis and hearing from God, a person cannot help but to be changed, just like Ehud.

JUST DO IT

As I write this book, I am fully aware of the fact that my job of parenting remains unfinished. At times during my writing, I felt like stopping, because I knew I wasn't the parent I needed to be for my children. Yet, I realized this book is not about me and it might encourage or perhaps even have the potential for changing someone's life. Therefore, I want you to know that I'm still in the battle. I feel woefully inadequate most days. I am just a father and a husband who is daily relying on the Holy Spirit of God to help me and give direction and guidance as I read the Bible and pray for insight and wisdom. I can do nothing on my own. I'm totally dependent on the Lord God. A branch can do nothing without being part of the vine. Jesus is the vine and I'm simply a branch. Apart from him, I can do nothing (see John 15:1-8).

This intentional process of making disciples in our homes is time-consuming and at times very arduous. All parents face those days that lead to much discouragement and turmoil. The hormone issues, which affect our children and the problems inherent with life can cause them to seem insane, which almost drives us to the brink of insanity ourselves. Sometimes we all feel like giving up, because we've had enough. But this is a job we cannot quit. Often I read these encouraging words of the Apostle Peter in 2 Peter 1:3: "His divine power has granted to us all things that pertain to life and godliness, through the knowledge of him who called us to his own glory and excellence…" God's power has given us all we need in this life to live godly lives through our knowledge in him. We can do it! Yes, it's hard going against the grain, but in Christ we are more than conquerors and we can do all things. So, we press on!

·5

How to Implement ROP

PATIENCE

As you begin this chapter, I'm assuming you have read the preceding chapters. However, I understand some may have skipped all of that and just want to get to the nuts and bolts of how to implement ROP in your home and/or church. I sincerely want to encourage you, if the latter describes your circumstances, to go back and read the preceding chapters. If you don't, you will likely be treating the biblical concept of *Rite of Passage* as just another program. You will attempt to implement it into your family life or church life and you may see no lasting changes for you or your people. I tell you this because we all want a quick fix. Please don't be tempted to try this with ROP. As I described in detail in chapter 3, this is *not* another program. Instead ROP is a lifestyle. If it is seen in this light, there is a much better likelihood that its implementation can be successful.

If you are a church leader, please know everyone will not understand or buy into ROP. Do not be offended or frustrated if they do not. I have found this to be the case in my own church. Not everyone is in the same place in their spiritual walk. It takes time and patience and much teaching on the subject. In fact, before I ever attempted to implement ROP in our church, I taught on the subject for several weeks. I preached through a sermon series on the family and the roles of the family members. I spoke about the role of the father, mother, child and parents. People must have time to process information, especially if it is new to them.

Today, even in the church, so much of our teaching regarding children, teenagers and young adults comes from a secular point of view. Sadly, we tend to listen more to talk show hosts, our friends and family about such things than we do the Bible. Getting information from those sources is quicker and easier than studying the Scriptures. However, in this case, there are no drive-thru windows at the ROP restaurant. Because of misinformation, traditions or unbiblical models, please know that when you begin teaching on the subject of family and Scriptural roles and the principles of running a godly home, you may get some strange or perplexed looks. Be prepared for those and understand those reactions are normal and should be anticipated. The Holy Spirit will do the work of changing hearts and minds. If you are a church leader, be patient and let the Holy Spirit do what you can't do. The same is true in our homes with our children and spouses. Can ROP be successful? Most definitely it can, but it takes time, much prayer and much patience.

If you are a parent, the same holds true for you as well. Be patient. As a parent myself, I recognize the difficulty in teaching and training children. It's by far the hardest and yet, most rewarding work I've ever done. Each and every child is different. Even children growing up in the same home can be markedly different in the way they react to discipline and training by parents depending upon how they are natured. I find this in my own home as well. Yet, with much prayer, time and patience, we can see positive results in our homes. Only in time can we tell how successful we have been in raising our children. Yet, along the way, we should have indications of how things are going by the behavior and attitudes exhibited by our children. Will we persevere? Will we contend for the faith? We will need to roll up our sleeves, swallow hard, hit our knees, study and teach the Bible. There is a direct correlation to the amount of time a family spends in the Word of God together, to the overall success of raising godly children. Again, all of this takes time. Rome wasn't built in a day.

CHANGED CULTURE

The information shared in the remainder of this chapter will be for the local church. This information will give the local church the ability to teach and implement ROP. As I began the process of implementing ROP in my home church, I taught for several weeks about the family, proper roles within the home and how to use Scripture to train our children. Slowly, over time, I began to see changes in families. Dads and moms began coming to me and telling me they wanted to know how to teach and train their children to become godly young adults in their homes. The conversations were heart-felt and sincere. I began to see a change in the cultural mind-set of the church. As I taught from many passages of Scripture, including: Psalms 78, Luke 2, Psalm 127, Deuteronomy 6, Ephesians 6, Hebrews 12, Titus 2, Matthew 17, and 3 John 4, to name a few, I witnessed the supernatural power of the Bible in changing our thinking. Parents were growing hungrier for biblical teaching they could share with their children. Intuitively, dads and moms know and recognize the responsibility inherent in being a parent and raising children to be godly. There are so many voices that whisper in our minds what we should and shouldn't do that it is difficult to navigate this mine field of uncertainty. I felt a huge responsibility and burden as a pastor to assist the people in this way. I began praying about what I could do to develop a way for parents and children to work through a process that was biblically based and yet simple enough to engage families. Over several weeks of praying, the Lord impressed upon my heart and mind a succinct process that I could use to lead in this way.

ROP-THE MODEL

As I studied Scripture, I recognized Jesus Christ is our model in all things, even as a 12-year-old. If he is our model for sacrifice at age 33, then he is our model at all ages of life. Thus, the 12-year-old Jesus is the example for our children. It's at that age we should begin expecting our children to begin behaving and thinking like young adults. I wanted to provide an opportunity for the families in the church to learn more about this model and how it applies to the concept of ROP. Jesus, at age 12, was thinking like a young adult. He knew he had to be about his Father's business. Our children should also be about the Father's – God's – business at age 12, generally speaking. Understanding the training and process of being about God's business is the essence of ROP. I informed the church through our weekly bulletin, email and via our website about an upcoming luncheon, after a Sunday service, where I would give information to those who might be interested in learning more.

I publicized the luncheon for about two months. I indicated in the correspondence to the church that any family having a young adult between the ages of 12 through 18 could attend. The church provided a spaghetti dinner. At this meeting I went into greater detail about ROP and what it entailed. I distributed a letter to each of the interested families. I even made the letters available ahead of time at our information desks for those families who were trying to decide if they even wanted to come to the luncheon. This letter can be found in Appendix 1, *Sample ROP Letter to Families*. In the letter I described ROP and the process we would go through, which would ultimately culminate in a special banquet and church service recognizing our ROP participants for that year.

Many families came to the luncheon and listened with much interest. I found dads and moms sincerely desiring to know how to encourage their children to be Christ-centered. The letter to the families also described a timeline for how ROP would work in the church setting. ROP can be done in the individual home as well. I encourage you, the reader, to own the concept of ROP whether or not your church ever becomes a ROP church. One of my desires in writing this book is to encourage churches to help the families within their congregations, but not every church will see ROP as the best way to do so. Families can choose to teach and train the children in the home by using the information available in this book.

In our situation ROP works very well in the spring of the year, graduation season. We have the introductory meeting in March, followed by the banquet in late April or early May and then conclude with the recognition ceremony during a Sunday morning worship service in mid-May. Keeping the schedule within a window of about 2 ½ months has proved to be helpful because working through the preparation questions becomes a priority. By nature, some people procrastinate. Giving people six months to work through this process might appear to be advantageous; yet in the long run, it seems that many wait until the last few weeks to do the work. Each church and family should decide what works best for them and their own calendars.

ROP PREPARATION QUESTIONS

Over the years I have developed a list of 20 preparation questions for our ROP participants to answer. These questions are found in Appendix 2. When you read the questions you will find there are actually more questions buried within the twenty. The goal is to get young adults digging into Scripture and seeking to understand what it means biblically to be godly in an ungodly world. I encourage parents to help their young adults with these questions, but they shouldn't do the work for them. Doing this helps no one. Parents can and should help, encourage and instruct through the process. Answering these questions takes several hours, (8 to 10 hours in most cases). This process takes a lot of time because of the amount of Bible study and verse look-ups required. It's true, a young adult can skip all the passages and answer the questions without reading them, but one can quickly tell if they have. You will quickly know that their motives in being a part of ROP are not genuinely pure.

I do not grade or mark what the participants give me. I simply review their answers to make sure they grasp the content and context of the Scriptures. If there appears to be some uncertainty about an answer or they seem confused, then I seek to help the participant and the parents in this area. It is fairly easy to tell if a young adult has truly invested the time and effort in answering the questions. Again, I don't review their answers as a teacher or professor. I don't grade for grammar or spelling either. I look at the content to see if I, as an elder, feel confident that this young adult understands the biblical guidelines and principles of what it means to be a young adult. This doesn't have to be checked by a pastor or leader, but should be reviewed by someone outside the family with Bible knowledge.

I try to encourage, compliment and build up our young adults in this process. It's a tremendous way to affirm young people, just as graduation does for high school students. As you review the questions in their entirety in Appendix 2, you may notice there are some thought-provoking questions. I have written the questions in a way to challenge young people to see if they sincerely grasp what the Bible says about growing up and putting aside childish ways. First and foremost, it is important to make certain they understand what it means to be a Christian. The questions seek to determine if they truly know what it means to be a follower of Jesus Christ, more than in name only. On one occasion a young man was going through the questions during the ROP process and he realized he needed to make certain of his salvation and commitment to Christ.

After reviewing the answers to the preparation questions, I return them to the young adult at the ROP Banquet for them to keep. The questions I have provided are what I've chosen to use. I have tweaked them and refined them through the years; however, you may develop your own questions which fit your situation better. I've also had many parents say what a blessing it was to work through these ROP preparation questions with their young adults. One mother wrote me and said:

> As parents, we are striving to teach our children the biblical principles they need to be "in" the world, yet not "of." Having our pastor come alongside us to reinforce the concepts we're teaching in our home has

made a world of difference in cementing the foundation. The thought-provoking questions helped Coleman search himself and really nail down a few loose ends. We're glad Pastor Kevin challenged Coleman with hard questions. As a Christian man, he'll have to answer hard questions about his faith for the rest of his life. This was wonderful preparation.

Another mother wrote:

I was so thankful that Allison had this opportunity and acted upon it. I feel she was blessed by it, in the time she put forth to study and write about the questions. It made her look inward and voice her convictions and love for the Lord. This is something she can refer back to later and hopefully see growth from then to now.

These testimonials stir my soul. I'm grateful to have the opportunity as a father and pastor to raise the bar in my home and in the church. Being challenged on a spiritual level is something most young people crave and desire. It has been exciting over the years to watch the metamorphosis that has taken place in the lives of young people. There is a wonderful bond which develops because of the shared experience of working many hours to tackle these deep and introspective questions.

THE BANQUET

One of the most rewarding things about ROP is the camaraderie *between* families and certainly *within* the families at our banquet. The banquet is a time of celebration for the participants in ROP that year. I have inserted a "Sample Banquet Ceremony" in Appendix 3. Typically for the banquet, we rent a large room at a local restaurant. The church covers the cost for the meal for the participants and their immediate families. If you have the space and the availability, the banquet can be held at your church with a catered meal. One way to make the meal less expensive is to have each family bring several covered dishes. Whatever you choose, make it a special time. The banquet should be a memorable experience for the families and young adults involved.

I encourage our families to dress up for the banquet. There is something about getting all dressed up to go to a function that gives it the feel of being important and special. I ask the young men to put on a tie and the ladies to wear modest dresses. The young adults really like getting dressed up. They have told me through the years that it makes them feel like something special is happening. The truth is *something special* is happening! We are celebrating the fact they have chosen to do something challenging and difficult because they desire to be godly and Christ-centered young adults. That is something worth celebrating!

We enjoy a great time of fellowship during the meal together and then I offer a charge to the participants. Typically I share a brief message from 1 Timothy 4:12 and/or 1 Corinthians 13:11. In this I challenge the young adults to live wholeheartedly with Jesus as the Lord of their lives. After I conclude, I give each of them a book which I have selected to encourage and grow them spiritually.

One of the things I ask parents to do to make the banquet experience personal and meaningful is to write a letter to their child who is participating in ROP. I ask parents to take the time to make the letter hand-written because it is much more personal than a typed letter. In the letter I encourage each parent to describe his or her own Christian journey and offer words of wisdom, advice and encouragement. During the banquet, the parents read these letters to their children at their individual tables. This is an intimate time between families. Often, during this special time of sharing, many tears are shed. It is wonderful to watch fathers and mothers and even older siblings read their letters. These moments are indelibly etched into the minds of the young adults. I know what the experience has meant to my wife and me, as we've had the privilege of sharing ROP with our two oldest daughters, Katy and

Kandace. I also encourage parents to ask grandparents or aunts and uncles to write letters. Many parents ask pastors, coaches, teachers and other role models or influential adults in their children's lives to write letters as well. Many participants have told me they cherish these letters and consider them to be a highlight of ROP.

A recent ROP participant gives compelling testimony about these letters. He writes:

> One of the most compelling parts of ROP was the letters I received from my family. My mother and I were talking about ROP just yesterday, and she was lamenting over how she wishes she had some connection to her grandmother, a major player in the molding of her childhood. Her grandmother passed away some eighteen years ago, and I can tell you, she would give anything to have a letter of admonition and wisdom directed to her from that godly woman. I never realized until then just how priceless these letters from my family are. These letters remind me of the books of the Bible, 1st and 2nd Timothy, in which the apostle Paul instructs and talks to the young man he'd mentored for so long. Timothy surely held onto these letters in times of distress and uncertainty after Paul had passed on, regarding them as a last connection to his former mentor. He probably looked at them when he had a difficult decision to make, and searched through their words and instructions to find out "what Paul would do in this situation." I now realize the worth of these letters. I'll always have a connection with my mentors; my father, my mother, my uncle and my grandparents. Even after they're gone, I will still have something left of them. I'll still have their heart on a page, written in their own distinctive handwriting; a permanent revelation from

my elders in the form of a letter penned on paper. In times of trouble, I know their words will always be there.

We conclude the banquet with prayer, lots of hugs and kisses and plenty of pictures. The ROP banquet is truly a memorable and delightful experience for all involved. I personally look forward to our annual banquet when a new group of young adults graduate through ROP.

THE RECOGNITION CEREMONY

There is something powerful when the body of Christ gets together to celebrate. The ROP Recognition Ceremony can certainly be one of those moments. As a church, we make a concerted effort to give much attention and prominence to our ROP participants each year. Most churches celebrate and congratulate the high school graduates annually. We do so as well, but how much more important is it to celebrate with young adults and their families as they emerge into Christian young adulthood? It is a wonderfully joyous and happy occasion when our children graduate academically and the same should be true when they "graduate" from childhood to young adulthood. The "graduation" which we establish the most emphasis is the one which our children will work toward with greatest fervor. Therefore, we devote an entire Sunday morning service to our ROP Recognition Ceremony.

There is a sample transcript of a "ROP Recognition Service" in Appendix 4. Prior to the service we invite the participants' immediate and extended family to attend the service. The reason we devote an entire service each year to our young adults is to show them how important they are to the life of the church. It is evident during this celebration that our church puts great emphasis on ROP and we believe it is a monumental step in a young person's life.

I present a brief message and remind the church about why we do ROP and the role the church plays in supporting our families and young adults. The church provides a certificate to each participant and we recognize them publicly. We also give them an opportunity to share a word of testimony with the church. While sharing a testimony is not required, it is highly recommended. I often remind our young people that if they are expected to give reports and presentations in classes at school, we really should expect no less at church. These testimonies are usually short, but moving. Normally participants share something that happened to them during the ROP process. Often, their testimonies include something about one or two of the preparation questions they answered or even something that was written to them by a parent or grandparent. These testimonies are a highlight of the ceremony.

PASSING THE BATON

At the conclusion of the testimonies, I ask all the participants and any family members present to come forward and line up across the front of the church. As they do, I hand each father a genuine track baton. The track baton is an anodized baton that can be purchased online in bulk. They are very inexpensive, around $3 each, including shipping costs, but very beautiful. These batons become a keepsake for all the participants and many tell me they place them in their rooms as a reminder of their commitments to follow Christ as Lord. What we do next is purely symbolic, but very powerful. I ask the young adults to stand in front of their fathers, or someone they choose if the father is not available or absent. The fathers take the batons and pass them. During this moment I explain the hand-off's symbolism from Paul's description of running the race in 2 Timothy 4:7. It is difficult to describe the emotions of this moment in a book, but the smiles that come over the faces of the young men and young women once they grasp those batons are something to behold! At this point, I invite the church to share their appreciation and each year a standing ovation ensues. It is a wonderful and blessed event! We conclude the service with prayer and a luncheon. What an amazing picture this is of the body of Christ growing together!

WHAT NOW?

After the ceremony ROP doesn't end. In many respects it really just begins. The leadership in the church begins to plug these young adults into the life of the church. Involvement is truly the key. The young, or anyone for that matter, learn best by doing, not by being entertained. We must involve our young people in the religious life of our homes and churches. We should give them a role in the family devotions. Each one should have his or her own Bible and participate fully in the Bible study and in Scripture memorization. Over time, they should grow in their knowledge and understanding of Scripture so they become equipped to lead discussions about the Bible. They should begin seeing themselves as a significant part of God's family and contributors to their home and church. ROP is simply a process for seeing those goals attained.

The ROP preparation questions help us to see where the young adult may have a desire to serve in the church. We ask the following:

√   What is it that you sense the Lord desires for you to do to become an active participant in this church?

√   How has God gifted you that you may be used to further his work in this church and this community?

We discuss theses desires with the young adults and seek to incorporate them into the various functions and ministries of the church. (See chapter 3 for more detail on the role of the church in ROP.) During our first ROP, we had a young man who said he was interested in learning how to work our audio-visual system. At the time this young man was 13-years-old, so there was some hesitancy on behalf of the main operator of our audio-visual system. He understood what we were doing with ROP, but was a little concerned, nonetheless. (Our audio-visual system was and is an expensive system.) Ultimately, he began mentoring our young 13-year ROP graduate and within a few weeks the young man could run the system almost by himself. In fact, presently, this young man is so proficient with the audio-visual system, he is asked to come run it by himself, without an "adult," for many church functions.

I want to share with you a quick story about this young man and the power of ROP when someone is involved in the life of the church. During the summer, right after ROP, the young man's father took him to his grandmother's to stay for a few days while there was no school. The father called on Saturday and asked if he'd like to stay a few more days. The son said, "No way Dad! Come and get me! I've got to be at church tomorrow to help run the A/V system!" How many 13-year-old boys do you know who are begging to come to church? He had ownership in the church because he had been given responsibility. The power of mentorship and raising the bar of expectations within a church can be very powerful. The entire church culture will change if you choose to implement ROP, and what a change it is. The church becomes one, not segregated. The entire body functions together, as it is intended. Paul describes the wonderful body of Christ beautifully in Ephesians 4:15-16 and sums ROP in these two verses:

Rather, speaking the truth in love, we are to grow up in every way into him who is the head, into Christ, from whom the whole body, joined and held together by every joint with which it is equipped, when each part is working properly, makes the body grow so that it builds itself up in love.

·6

Will ROP Work?

WHAT REALLY MATTERS?

Recently while searching for some old documents, I discovered some old pictures of my two teenage daughters. There they were in their pig tails with their big, bright eyes gleaming, and their little baby teeth sparkling through massive smiles. Where did those days go? Now those pig tails are gone, replaced with long, flowing hair and those baby teeth and eyes that looked almost too big for their faces have been replaced by the smiles of young adults. Life has a way of sneaking past us without us knowing it. While the children are little we take for granted their hugs and kisses when we walk through the door. Yet all too soon, those days are quickly replaced with empty houses and fewer place settings at the dinner table. I look at my oldest girls and know that one day, sooner than I can even imagine, they will be gone. When that day comes, and it most definitely will come, will they be prepared? Will they have been trained and equipped and be living as young adults who have centered their lives on Christ or will they be floundering around in a world that is waiting to chew them up and spit them out?

Right now my children are all still in the home. They still live under my roof, my protection, my provision, my watch-care and my spiritual leadership. I have the opportunity every day to make decisions which will either benefit or hamper their spiritual growth. What really matters when it comes to my children in the light of eternity? What really matters when it comes to your children in the light of eternity? When all is said and done, what really matters in the life of anyone? The Bible says that what matters is what we have done with God's son, Jesus Christ. We either accept the fact that he is the son of God, who was raised to life after being crucified on a cross for our sins, and teach this fact, live by this fact, and run our lives by this fact or we reject it. ROP is a way of living a lifestyle in the home. ROP is a term I've used to describe a biblical philosophy that begins at birth and ends at adulthood for our children. This passage is more of a season of opportunity in which we have the chance to pass the baton of our faith in Christ to our children than it is a date that we can put on a calendar.

Our children are learning from us every day. They see what is important to us by where we spend our time and how we spend our money. Billy Graham once said you can look at a person's calendar and checkbook and tell quickly what he or she values and holds dear. What kind of legacy do we want to leave our children? How will they remember us? Did we choose to live in a way that pointed them to Christ, enough to impact the way they choose to live? The clock is ticking. It stops for no one. There are no timeouts in life. Often, we must make decisions on the fly and then live with those decisions as we look back at them as snapshots in time. What will those pictures look like? What will we see? Hopefully we see pictures of our family sitting in the family room or around the kitchen table studying the Bible together. Maybe we will see children learning and memorizing Scripture. Could it be that we might see an empty home because the family is seldom there? Is it possible we could see a home where the family is living separate lives under the same roof with everyone doing their own thing? Time is happening right now. It is slipping into the future.

ARROWS

Many have asked me over the years if ROP works. My short answer is: "Yes and no." Yes, ROP works if you see it as a lifestyle choice and you live with a single-minded focus of following

Scripture and living by it. No, ROP doesn't work if you see it simply as an 8-week block on a calendar in the spring after your child's 12th birthday where you run through a church program like a car goes through a car wash. ROP works not because it is something new or hip. It works because it points us back to the ancient paths of raising children consistently, diligently and with pin-point focus on the things of God.

The Bible teaches that children are like arrows in our hands. The Bible records the admonition of the Psalmist in Psalm 127:3-4:

> *Behold, children are a heritage from the LORD, the fruit of the womb a reward. Like arrows in the hand of a warrior are the children of one's youth. Blessed is the man who fills his quiver with them!*

This is a wonderful metaphor. My four children are like arrows in my hand and I have the privilege to train, equip and ultimately pull them from my quiver and shoot them. Where will they go? Will they shoot straight? Much of this is up to me. ROP occurs when they are still in the quiver. If I've done my job, then there is great likelihood they will sail long and straight and true toward the mark, the goal and high calling of Christ.

Unless the Lord Builds the House

How do we go about making sure our children are arrows that are shot straight and sure? In the first verse of Psalm 127, we are told:

> *Unless the LORD builds the house, those who build it labor in vain. Unless the LORD watches over the city, the watchman stays awake in vain.*

This verse embodies the purpose of ROP. Unless the Lord builds the house, we labor in vain. The Lord God must build the house and Jesus Christ must be the rock foundation on which we build that house. A house is not built overnight. It takes months and in some cases, years to build a home. Our children are built and developed over many years of teaching and training. How are we building the lives of our children? What are we building into their lives? As fathers, these questions must be answered honestly and with prayerful introspection. Philip Lancaster in his book, *Family Man, Family Leader: Biblical Fatherhood as the Key to a Thriving Family* sums up these sentiments (Lancaster, 294).

Those of us who live in modern America (and similar lands) live in a giant slum, speaking in terms of the condition of our family life. The physical houses are, for the most part, structurally sound and reasonably attractive on the outside, but the families that inhabit them have deteriorated over the years to the point where they are barely holding together, if they are at all. Even the best of them are only a shell of what families once were, since the members of the household have little meaningful life together, and they are not fulfilling the callings God has given fathers, mothers, and children. They are badly in need of restoration.

These are sobering words, yet true. We must honestly look at our lives and our schedules and ask ourselves what our houses look like from a foundational level. Are we trying to cover and hide cracks with a façade of religion or are they strongly built on the Word of God? Will we make the necessary repairs that lead to restoration?

As a pastor, I sometimes look at the world and ask myself, "How can we fix our churches and ultimately this nation and repair all of these families?" Lancaster shares an encouraging answer to this daunting question when he writes (Lancaster, 295):

> The need is utterly overwhelming when viewed overall. But the solution is well within reach when viewed from the standpoint of each household. A father doesn't have to fix the whole society; he just has to fix his own family. And here is the amazing and hopeful thing about God's national rebuilding plan: *the renewal strategy that is within the reach of each father—making changes in his own home—is the strategy that*

will have the greatest overall effect for the kingdom of God. As each of us sees to our own little sphere of dominion, our own families, the combined effect will be renewed communities, churches, and nations. (Emphasis his)

My heart almost skips a beat when I read those words because of what could happen if we decide to get serious and make the necessary changes in our homes. The great puritan churchman, Richard Baxter preached reformation in the 1600's. Still today, his words ring true. Baxter writes (Baxter, 21):

> You are not likely to see any general reformation, till you procure family reformation. Some little religion there may be here and there; but while it is confined to single persons, and is not promoted in families, it will not prosper, nor promise future increase.

The reality is unless we radically change the way we view the role of the family in the church and the home, we will not see an end to the systematic decimation of both institutions. We will either win the culture back one family at a time or we will lose the culture one family at a time. It is that simple. Either way we look at it, the family is the key. Until we have a vision for multigenerational faithfulness in our homes and churches, we will continue to lose the battle of raising Christ-centered young adults. ROP gives us an avenue by which we may live out that multigenerational vision.

FEW THERE BE THAT FIND IT

When Jesus preached on the earth he had thousands of people following him. When he ascended to heaven and the believers were assembled in Jerusalem, there were only 120. Amazing isn't it? Only 120 true believers could be found after three years of preaching, teaching, healing and miracles. Jesus said that the way is narrow and *few there be that find it*. ROP is that way. It's a narrow passage. Few will choose this path because it is hard. Most people don't like doing hard things. We'd rather find the easy way out or take the short-cut. There are no short-cuts in this journey. It is a long and hard climb up a mountain of many obstacles. The Bible says in Hebrews 5:7-9:

> *During the days of Jesus' life on earth, he offered up prayers and petitions with fervent cries and tears to the one who could save him from death, and he was heard because of his reverent submission. Son though he was,* he learned obedience from what he suffered *and, once made perfect, he became the source of eternal salvation for all who obey him. (Emphasis added)*

Jesus learned obedience by *suffering*. It isn't fun to suffer. Who wants to suffer? Most of us want it easy and each successive generation tries to make things better for the next. But what if our children have to suffer because of a bad economy or even persecution? Are we training our children to endure suffering? Are we training them to be strong in the face of potential persecution? Will they remain, endure and persevere? Can they do hard things? Can they live on less than they grew up with or will they sell their souls for material wealth, comfort and prosperity? Will they *remain* in the faith if one day being a Christian actually costs them something—even their lives?

The Apostle John wrote his little epistle of 1 John to help identify the marks of a true believer (see 1 John 5:13). In 1 John 2:19 the Apostle said: "They went out from us, but they were not of us; for if they had been of us, they would have continued with us. But they went out, that it might become plain that they all are not of us." The key word in that verse is *continued*. Who are true believers? We addressed this question in detail in chapter 2, but it truly is the critical question. Jesus had many followers prior to his arrest. Later, after his death, only 120 remained. What happened to the rest? They were not truly believers. They did not *continue*.

I have constant conversations with my children about Christianity and genuine salvation and what it looks like in the life of a sincere believer. Being a believer in Christ is more than just words we say; it is a lifestyle that is lived. I want my children to know and understand what the Scripture says when it comes to *evidence* of salvation. Paul told the believers at Corinth to take a spiritual check-up. 2 Corinthians 13:4-6 records:

> *Examine yourselves, to see whether you are in the faith. Test yourselves. Or do you not realize this about yourselves, that Jesus Christ is in you?—unless indeed you fail to meet the test! I hope you will find out that we have not failed the test.*

We should make sure that we pass the test. And we should seek to do so with our children as well.

PRINCIPLES AND PROMISES

I sincerely believe we can raise godly children. I believe the principles outlined in Scripture and those I have detailed in this book give strong evidence that such is the case. Proverbs 22:6 says:

> *Train up a child in the way he should go; even when he is old he will not depart from it.*

This verse teaches that if we raise our children in the way they are "bent" by God, then even when old, they will not depart from the faith. That is a Scriptural principle, which means there doesn't have to be a season of "sowing wild oats;" instead, the young person will continue or remain in the faith from childhood all the way up to and through old age. But is it a guarantee? Is it a promise? I don't believe it is.

But, we want guarantees don't we? We buy products with money-back guarantees. We buy cars with warranties. Can we know for certain, if we raise our children following the principles of Scripture and do all the right spiritual things that we are guaranteed to have Christ-centered adults? Even in writing this book, I have wrestled with this question. For now, until the Lord shows me differently in Scripture, I'm prepared to say there are no 100% guarantees in raising children. Why? The reason is because children have a choice. We live in a fallen world that is racked with sin and thus we are all born sinful. Sin carries its own penalty and punishment—spiritual death. However, inherently with sin comes a choice. Our children can choose to obey or disobey. They will have to make up their own minds if they are going to choose to submit their wills, hearts, souls and minds to Christ. As much as we would like to, we simply cannot do this for them.

If we examine Scripture closely, we find that even godly fathers raised wicked sons. Conversely, there were godly sons that rose up from wicked and vile fathers (see 1 and 2 Kings). I know some will read the last couple of paragraphs and say, "Wait a minute, you seem to be saying this endeavor of raising Christ-centered children is like rolling the dice or luck of the draw." This is not my intention. I'm fully prepared to say I trust unequivocally in the principles of Scripture, but I will not make promises where I do not see them.

Can anyone guarantee a child at birth will one day be a Christ-following, dedicated saint of God? I don't believe it is possible. Abel obeyed, while Cain rebelled. Yet, they grew up in the same home. The same was true with Jacob and Esau. The former trusted, while the latter sold out. David, a man after God's own heart believed till the end, while Solomon, his son, walked away in his old age. Look at the life of Judas. Not even the other apostles knew who he really was even up to the point of the betrayal of Christ. Yet, they all ate, slept and lived side by side for over three years. We have all seen or known children who grew up in godly homes where one or more trusted Christ and others walked away. Same home, but different results. Much could be said about the overall training in those homes, perhaps. We can speculate that maybe there were deficiencies. But, it really all comes down to the *grace of God*. We simply do all we can and leave the rest to him. Paul said that it is by grace we have been saved through faith, not of works so that no one can boast. Knowing Christ is not of works, but is by the grace of God and his good pleasure. Paul also said in Philippians 2:12-13:

> *Therefore, my beloved, as you have always obeyed, so now, not only as in my presence but much more in my absence, work out your own salvation with fear and trembling, for it is God who works in you, both to will and to work for his good pleasure.*

WHAT IF THEY WALK AWAY?

You may be reading this book and you have children who have walked away. Now the most important thing you can do for them is *pray*. There are some things that only the Holy Spirit can accomplish. I encourage you to *fast and pray* for their salvation. Do not try to convince yourself that they know Christ if you aren't 100% convinced. Perhaps they do, but if they have walked away and give no evidence of Christian fruit in their lives, then it is better to pray as if they do not. Satan has deceived many parents into thinking their children know the Lord because they prayed a prayer or were baptized as a child. That is a dangerous assumption.

Some of you, however, know your child has rejected taking the baton of faith and are sinning against God. You may even feel that your own reputation has been damaged. You might angrily say, "Can't they see what this is doing to me?" In your mind you think, "I raised my child better than this! What happened?" But, as parents, we must see our investment into the lives of our children in the *light of eternity*. If we focus on the short term, we will likely have our own pity-party and make their lack of salvation all about us. However, those who make the greatest difference are those who continue to invest without the expectation of immediate return. Galatians 6:9 says, "And let us not grow weary of doing good, for in due season we will reap, *if we do not give up*." We all know stories of those who left the faith and went through a prolonged season of darkness, yet eventually emerged in the light. Maybe this is your personal story. Have faith that this will be your son's or daughter's story as well.

In his book *Handoff*, Jeff Myers shares (Myers, 143-44):

> I've often wondered where Jesus got the patience and perspective to put up with all of the guff his followers gave him. The answer that appears in Scripture is so simple that I rejected it out of hand the first time I heard it. Jesus surrendered the outcome to God. To surrender the outcome to God means acting

faithfully through the *process*, but relinquishing control of the *results*. My goal in passing the baton is to make sure the pass takes place...then I can release any worry about whether the person I hand off to wins the race. As long as I feel responsible for the outcome of the lives of others, I live in worry. I fret about whether my kids will turn out all right. But when I surrender the outcome to God, fear melts away. (Emphasis his)

I wholeheartedly agree with Mr. Myers. There is a wonderful passage of Scripture found in 2 Peter 1:3-9 which provides immense comfort to me as a parent.

His divine power has granted to us all things that pertain to life and godliness, through the knowledge of him who called us to his own glory and excellence, by which he has granted to us his precious and very great promises, so that through them you may become partakers of the divine nature, having escaped from the corruption that is in the world because of sinful desire. For this very reason, make every effort to supplement your faith with virtue, and virtue with knowledge, and knowledge with self-control, and self-control with steadfastness, and steadfastness with godliness, and godliness with brotherly affection, and brotherly affection with love. For if these qualities are yours and are increasing, they keep you from being ineffective or unfruitful in the knowledge of our Lord Jesus Christ. For whoever lacks these qualities is so nearsighted that he is blind, having forgotten that he was cleansed from his former sins.

In his book *Age of Opportunity*, Paul David Tripp gives keen insight and encouragement to parents in this passage. Tripp writes (Tripp, 104-05):

Peter says, "Don't forget who you are. You are the children of God who have inherited riches beyond your ability to conceive. You have been given everything you need to do what God has called you to do. Don't give in to discouragement. Don't quit. Don't run away from your calling." We need to walk into the rooms of our children saying to ourselves, "I have everything I need to do what God has called me to do." This is our identity as the children of God. These are the truths that can lift us out of our weariness and discouragement to parent with faith, courage, and hope. They call us to hold onto God's high goals and to fight the hopelessness that the enemy wants to rule our hearts.

We are not alone! God has equipped us to do the job. The Bible says we can parent with hope! When those times come where we feel like throwing in the towel, when we are at the end of our rope, we must hold on to what the Bible teaches us. We have all we need in Christ and we are more than conquerors in him. We must keep on moving forward to the high calling of Christ and we will persevere!

EYES ON ETERNITY

What kind of stewards are we being of our children? We must be faithfully training and teaching them and not pursuing other things that won't matter in eternity. Children are eternal. I know this is a simple statement, but we must grasp the enormity of it. Read it again in isolation.

Children are eternal.

Our children are going to live forever. They will live forever in either heaven or hell. Jesus said that we should store up our treasures in heaven. Other than Christ, what greater treasure could there be in heaven than our children? Yet, it is so easy to lose eternal focus for temporal things. We know we should set our minds on things above, but we get distracted by the stuff of this earth. ROP living is really *kingdom living*. Therefore, if the truth be known, we are not trying to pass our children into adulthood alone, but ultimately right into the kingdom of heaven.

   Is ROP the answer to all of our problems as parents and those
who work with young adults? I have already stated that it is not.
However, if we choose to embrace the principles outlined in
Scripture, we have a great opportunity for success. What is success?
To raise genuine, Christ-centered, soldiers who are willing to
contend for the faith. May that endeavor be our passion and our
greatest joy. And may we one day say with immense satisfaction:
"I have no greater joy than to hear that my children are walking in
the truth" (3 John 4).

For Further Reading

Barna Group, "Most Twentysomethings Put Christianity on the Shelf Following Spiritually Active Teen Years." http://www.barna.org/barna-update/article/16-teensnext-gen/147-most-twentysomethings-put-christianity-on-the-shelf-following-spiritually-active-teen-years, 2006 (accessed May 13, 2011).

Baucham, Jr., Voddie T. *Family Driven Faith: Doing What It Takes to Raise Sons and Daughters Who Walk with God.* Wheaton, Illinois: Crossway Books, 2007.

Baxter, Richard. *The Reformed Pastor.* Edinburgh, Scotland: Banner of Truth, 1979.

Black, David Alan. *The Myth of Adolescence.* Yorba Linda, California: Davidson Press, 1999.

Freudenburg, Fred and Rick Lawrence. *The Family-Friendly Church.* Loveland, Colorado: Group Publishing, Inc., 1998.

Ham, Ken, and Frank Beemer. *Already Gone: Why Your Kids Will Quit Church and What You Can Do to Stop It.* Green Forest, Arkansas: New Leaf Publishing Group/Master Books, 2009.

Lancaster, Philip. *Family Man, Family Leader: Biblical Fatherhood as the Key to a Thriving Family.* San Antonio, Texas: The Vision Forum, Inc., 2004.

Myers, Jeffrey L. *Handoff: The Only Way to Win the Race of Life.* Dayton, Tennessee: Legacy Worldwide, 2008.

Schlect, Christopher. *Critique of Modern Youth Ministry.* Moscow, Idaho: Canon Press, 2007.

Time Magazine, "Grow Up? Not So Fast," 2005. http://www.
　　time.com/time/magazine/article/0,9171,1018089,00.html,
　　(Accessed December 28, 2010).

Tripp, Paul David. *Age of Opportunity: A Biblical Guide to Parenting Teens.*
　　Phillipsburg, New Jersey: Presbyterian and Reformed Publishing
　　Company, 2001.

Appendix A
Sample ROP Letter to Families

Rite of Passage (insert date)

Date

Dear Parents:

Thank you for taking time to attend this information luncheon to learn more about and discuss "Rite of Passage." As you probably have heard me share, a "Rite of Passage" (ROP) into adulthood is a powerful means of shaping young lives for God. It is a specific time when parents blend loving words and caring actions with the help of the church into a meaningful ceremony designed to leave a lasting memory and an indelible mark on young people's lives. This process can provide a stabilizing point for the rest of the young person's life. Perhaps most of all, it gives our young men and young women the tangible evidence and knowledge that their parents' blessing and the Lord's is upon them as they continue to grow and mature as young adults.

In order for your child to participate in Rite of Passage, he or she must be at least 12 years of age or still in high school prior to our ceremony on May 2nd. If you choose to allow your child to participate in this ROP, please understand there will be much work involved in preparation for the banquet and the special recognition ceremony service to come. Attached are 20 preparation questions that we expect your young man or young lady to complete and turn back into me by Sunday, April 18th. If this material is not turned in on time, he or she will not be allowed to participate in the banquet (on Saturday evening April 24th at the _____ Restaurant) or the special service to recognize them on Sunday, May 2nd. This may seem somewhat rigid; but please understand, I cannot think of a more significant or potentially "life changing" experience your child could possibly be involved other than coming to Christ.

What is it that we're hoping to accomplish with ROP?

√   To affirm the claims of Christ in his/her life
√   To discern and apply the true values of life according to Scripture and to be able to live by them
√   To experience the presence of Christ every day by having a consistent time of Bible study and prayer to the Lord
√   To be able to accept himself/herself as God created him/her and to take joy in this
√   To experience the love of others and to know how to give love to others by being mannerly, respectful and obedient to authority and particularly you, their parents
√   To be an exemplary role model so that other people will want to know the Lord Jesus because of his/her testimony

We, the church, will do all we can to integrate and include our young men and women into every facet of church life. We have done this by including them into our adult choir and placing them on committees as apprentices. They can also serve as ushers and greeters, help teach children's Sunday School/Bible Study classes, work with the mission groups on Wednesday nights, as well as work with our men's and women's groups. Please understand, we're not asking for our young people to become substitutes for adults. We recognize they are young adults and need training and mentoring. Rather, they are essential, complementary components to our more seasoned adults. They will learn what it means to truly be a Christian adult through this training and mentoring (Titus 2).

What I've described is basically an apprenticeship program that will involve and engage our young people into the life of the church. This process will enable them to have a better understanding of the basic ministries of the church and will cultivate within them an interest in using their talents for God. As parents, particularly fathers, you play the most significant role in raising your children to become godly young adults. Our desire, as the church, is to partner with you in this process. We believe the key is involvement. The young learn best by doing, not by being entertained. It is important to involve your young person in the religious life of your home. Give them a role in the family devotions. Each one should have his or her own Bible and participate fully in the Bible study and in Scripture memorization. Over time, they should grow in their knowledge and understanding of Scripture so they become equipped to lead discussions about the Bible. They should begin seeing themselves as a significant part of God's family and as making an important contribution to their home and church.

We believe we must return to what the Scriptures teach about raising our young people and dismiss the patterns of this world. In our culture no one seems to know when a young person is supposed to grow up. However, the Bible gives Jesus as our example as a 12-year-old in the temple saying, "Didn't you know I had to be about my Father's business?" We follow Christ's example and as a church we raise the bar of expectations for our young adults. We no longer want to watch a slow, steady decline in the commitment of our young people. We believe, as families, we can raise a generation of young people who will live for the Lord Jesus. Paul tells our young people, "Don't let anyone look down on you because you are young, but set an example for the believers in speech, in life, in love, in faith and in purity." (1 Tim. 4:12). Our goal is really nothing new. Instead, ROP is simply getting back to something that is old and that is tried and true when it comes to teaching, equipping and training our young people. We are simply returning to Scripture.

We are excited about our upcoming banquet, as mentioned above. This will be a semi-formal event. We encourage young men to wear a coat and tie if available and for the ladies to wear modest dresses. At the banquet, we will have a time of testimony, music and fellowship among families. I will share a brief charge to the participants as well. There will also be a time of sharing among individual families that will be very memorable.

To make the evening even more special, we are asking you, as parents, to do something special for your young adult. We would like to ask each parent to write a letter to your child telling him/her what the Lord has meant to you in your life through your own experiences with Him. In other words, tell him or her what your faith in Christ has meant to you. This would be a simple, heart-to-heart testimonial about the challenges of growing up and how the grace of God is sufficient to meet any challenges or needs. Also consider asking others who are close to your young person to do the same (i.e.; grandparents, older siblings or aunts/uncles, a coach, pastor, teacher, etc). You may want to include some family history for your child. Items such as copies of old family pictures of you and your parents and even grandparents or great-grandparents are wonderful. If you have any genealogies or family tree information, ROP is a good time to pull that information together as well. ROP serves as a great occasion to document your family heritage. Providing this family history of the men and women who came before your son or daughter will be a priceless keepsake.

You may want to purchase something nice for your young adult to keep these letters and documents in for protection. Perhaps a string-close, legal document holder or a small wooden box would serve the purpose. Your child will cherish these letters and photos forever. There will be a time during the banquet to present these items and for you, as parents, to read your letters to your young adult. (Note: The reading of these letters will take place at your table privately, while everyone else is doing the same at their table. Nothing is read publicly.)

Finally, on Sunday, May 2nd, we will have a special ceremony during the morning worship service. Your young adult will be asked to share something he or she learned from the ROP experience or his or her personal testimony. Depending on the number of participants, each will have about 2-3 minutes to share. It is good to write it down and practice it. At the end of the service, I will call our young men and women forward along with you, the parents, and the rest of any of your family who can attend. We will ask you to place your hands on your young adult and then I'll lead us in prayer for God's blessing upon him or her. The prayer will be a call for each to serve God mightily in their homes, this church and in their community. I would encourage you also at some point to consider taking your young person on a weekend outing. This can be a special time of learning, mentoring and sharing together. You could even go over the preparation questions with your child as a time of encouragement and challenge.

What a wonderful time of celebration and commitment ROP is for our church. We are so excited about what the Lord is doing to shape, mold and grow our children for his glory (Proverbs 4:11-12). To God be the glory! 3 John 4 says, "I have no greater joy than to hear my children are walking in the truth." Indeed, this is our desire for young adults!

Pastor Kevin

Appendix B
Sample ROP Preparation Questions

Parents, you are highly encouraged to assist your young adult(s) with reviewing and answering these questions, but do NOT do the work for them. They need to invest the time and energy into this process. They will reap in direct proportion to what they sow. If done with the proper priority, the investment they will make in answering these questions will prove to be rewarding for them and for your entire family. The process of answering these questions will take many hours. All Scripture references should be read and studied before attempting to answer the questions. If done properly, this process will require at least 8-10 hours, on average, to complete.

PREPARATION QUESTIONS

1. How does a person become a Christian, a born again believer and follower of Christ? Use Scripture references to support your answer. Also, describe in detail your salvation experience and what led to you surrendering your life to the Lordship of Christ. Please be detailed and specific.
2. Describe your relationship with Christ. Indicate what you are doing to grow in your knowledge and understanding of Christ. Indicate if you have a daily time of personal prayer and Bible study. In other words, when, where and

how do you spend time with the Lord? (Please note, if you are spending little or no time praying and reading your Bible, you are more than likely not ready to proceed with ROP at this time.)

3. What does it mean to act like and behave like an adult? (For the young man, please read: 1 Tim. 3:1-11, Judg. 3:12-30, 2 Tim. 2:22-25, Titus 1:6-9, Titus 2:1-8. For the young woman, please read: Prov. 31:10-31, 2 Tim. 2:22-25, Titus 2:1-8.)

4. Explain in your own words Luke 2:41-52 and the example set forth by Jesus in this passage.

5. What do you believe about the Bible? What role should reading the Scriptures on a consistent basis play in your life? Why? (See 2 Tim. 2:15, 2 Tim. 3:14-17.)

6. How do you know the Bible is truly the Word of God and not just another "holy" book like the Koran or the Book of Mormon? (See 1 Peter 1:20-21. I would also encourage you to google Josh McDowell's or Lee Strobel's websites for more information on Biblical apologetics.)

7. Please review in detail these Scriptures about heeding instruction and correction from your parents: Prov. 10:17, Prov. 12:1 and Prov. 15:32. What does it mean to be obedient and to honor your parents? (Eph. 6:1-3.) What is promised to you if you honor and obey your parents? Give examples of how you specifically honor your parents.

8. In light of your understanding of the passages listed in question #7, how should you speak to your parents and others (i.e., tone of voice, body language, facial expression, etc.)? Please see Prov. 15:1, Prov. 17:14, Prov. 30:17, James 1:19-20, Prov. 29:20, Prov. 17:28, Prov. 12:22.

9. What does the Bible say about parents disciplining their children? Please read the following Scriptures before answering: Heb. 12:5-11, Prov. 3:11, Prov. 12:1, Prov. 13:1, Prov. 13:18, Prov. 13:24, Prov. 15:10, Prov. 16:20, Prov. 19:18, Prov. 20:6, Prov. 22:6, Prov. 22:15, Prov. 23:13-14, Prov. 29:15-17).

10. After reading the following passages, explain what the Bible teaches about espousal, courtship, relationships and marriage. List each of these passages of Scripture specifically in your answer with explanations to follow. (1 Thess. 4:1-8, Matt. 1:18-25, Gen. 24, Gen. 39, Titus 2:14, Eph. 5:3, Gal. 6:7-10, 1 Cor. 10:13, 2 Cor. 11:2, Prov. 4:23, Prov. 5, Prov. 6:20-35, Prov. 7, Rom. 13:11-14, 1 Cor. 7, 1 Tim. 5:2, 2 Cor. 6:14-16, Eph. 5:21-33.) Parents I encourage you to consider reading Joshua Harris' books: "I Kissed Dating Goodbye," or "Boy Meets Girl," or Voddie Baucham's book: "What He Must Be."

11. After reading the following passages: Prov. 23:4-5, 2 Cor. 8:1-15, 2 Cor. 9:6-15, Luke 6:38, Matt. 6:19-34; Luke 12:13-21, 1 Tim. 6:6-10, 17-19: please answer these questions: What does it mean to be responsible with money? What can happen to a person who is greedy for money? Do you give of your money to God's work? Why or why not?

12. Is there a cost to following Christ? See Matt. 10:32-39, Matt. 16:24-26, Luke 14:25-35. Be specific please.

13. What does the Bible teach you are to do if you have offended someone (even if it's unknowingly)? See Matt. 5:21-26. What should you do if someone sins against you? See Matt. 18:15-20.

14. What type of friends should a young adult have? Answer in relation to the Scriptures recorded in Psalm 1, Prov. 13:20 and 1 Cor. 15:33.

15. What specific characteristics does the Bible say a young adult should have? See 1 Tim. 4:12, Psalm 119:9-11. (1 Tim. 4:12 is perhaps one of the most important Scriptures you will define and explain in the ROP process. I encourage you to memorize it.)

16. In light of the above question, write a detailed description of what it means to be a young man or young woman who is 100% committed to the Lordship of Jesus Christ in his or her life. In other words, what would that young person look like, act like, talk like and be like? Please think about your answer carefully. As you write the answer to this question, honestly evaluate if you are this kind of dedicated follower and disciple of Christ.

17. If you were told you were going to die in just two weeks, how would you spend the remainder of your life? What would you do? What specific changes or adjustments in your priorities do you need to make in order to draw closer to Christ and be what he wants you to be?

18. Statistics show 70% to 92% of all Christian young people, who were raised in church, will abandon their faith by their 20th birthday. Why do you think this is so and do you think this could happen to you? Why or why not?

19. What is it that you sense the Lord desires for you to do to become an active participant in this church? In other words, how has God gifted you that you may be used to further his work in this church and this community?

20. Discover your family history. Find out more about who you are by learning about where your great-grandparents were from and who they were. Document what you can find out about them. If possible, locate pictures of them and make copies of them. List something you didn't know about your family.

Appendix C
Sample Banquet Ceremony

Rite of Passage Banquet-(Date)

"When I was a child, I spoke like a child, I thought like a child, I reasoned like a child. When I became a man, I gave up childish ways" (1 Corinthians 13:11).

5:30 pm Catered Dinner or at a restaurant with private room
6:30 pm Charge from Pastor
7:00 pm Family Sharing Time (Sharing of letters, family history, photos, gifts)
8:00 pm Closing Prayer

Participants:
(List names of participants)

"I have no greater joy than to hear that my children are walking in the truth." 3 John 4

Appendix D
Sample ROP Recognition Service

Today is our annual Rite of Passage recognition service. Let me remind you about ROP and why we do ROP in our church. As I have shared before, ROP is a powerful means of shaping young lives for God. It is a specific time when parents blend loving words and caring actions with the help and partnership of the church. ROP is a process and journey that is designed to leave a lasting memory and an indelible mark on the lives of young people. ROP provides a stabilizing point for the rest of the young person's life. Perhaps most of all, it gives our young men and young women the tangible evidence and knowledge that their parents' blessing and the Lord's is upon them as they continue to grow and mature as young adults.

We follow the example of Jesus in Luke 2, where, at 12 years of age, Jesus knew exactly where he was headed and the ultimate purpose of life. He said, "Didn't you know I had to be about my Father's business?" In "being about the Father's business," Jesus was submissive to his parents. Luke 2:51 tells us He grew in wisdom and stature and favor with God and men. We follow Jesus' example…so at age 12, young people can participate in ROP here at our church.

Participating in and completing ROP means each young person is now accepted as an emerging young adult. It also means he or she is expected to accept accountability for mature actions and to assume adult responsibilities, because we know that maturity does not necessarily come with age, but with acceptance of responsibility.

These young adults have done a tremendous amount of work to get to this point. They successfully completed a rigorous packet of questions, a catechism of sorts; which had them digging in the Bible for hours. They answered a myriad of questions in great detail such as: How does a person become a Christian? What does it mean to act like and behave like a young adult? What role should reading the Bible play in your life? What does it mean to be obedient and honor your parents? What does it mean to be responsible with money? What does the Bible say about parental discipline? What should the nature of your speech be as a young man or woman? What would you do if you only had two weeks to live? Why do you think you will not be part of the 70%-92% which drops out of church and abandons their faith by their 20th birthday? Their answers were well-written and impressive! We are proud of their Biblical knowledge and their desire to learn and to become young adults who have centered their lives on Christ.

We would like to recognize this morning our ROP participants and we'd like for them to come to the front and stand as their names are called.

They are: _____

_____

These young people have fulfilled the requirements set forth by the Word of God to be considered young adults by completion of this program. I'd like for them now to have the opportunity to accept and repeat an oath of commitment to follow the Lord as a Christ-centered young adult. I'm going to read the oath and then they will respond as they desire.

"Today in the presence of my family, my church and my God, I commit to put behind me childish ways and serve the Lord with his leading and guidance as a young adult. I agree to follow the teaching of Scripture as Paul told Timothy (whom scholars tell us was a teenager) in 1 Timothy 4:12: "Don't let anyone look down on you because you are young, but set an example for the believers in speech, in life, in love, in faith and in purity.""

If you will commit to keeping this oath, would you now say, "I DO." Thank you very much!

The certificate reads as follows:

> *"Mount Pleasant Baptist Church awards this certificate to you, having completed the necessary work and spiritual training to be considered and deemed a young adult. The church congratulates and celebrates with you upon the successful completion of your "Rite of Passage" into adulthood. May Jesus Christ richly bless you as you journey through life with Him as your Lord and Savior."*

There is a verse on the certificate from 1 Corinthians 13:11 that says, "When I was a child, I spoke like a child, I thought like a child, I reasoned like a child. When I became a man, I gave up childish ways."

I would now like to ask the families to come and join their young adults so that we may pray a prayer of dedication over them. Please come forward and surround your young adult and place your hands on him or her as we pray together this prayer of dedication.

PRAYER OF DEDICATION

Listen to the words of the Psalmist (Psalm 78:3-7) as instructions are given on how we are to pass our faith in God to the next generation.

> *What we have heard and known, what our fathers have told us. We will not hide them from their children; we will tell the next generation the praiseworthy deeds of the LORD, his power, and the wonders he has done. He decreed statutes for Jacob and established the law in Israel, which he commanded our forefathers to teach their children, so the next generation would know them, even the children yet to be born, and they in turn would tell their children. Then they would put their trust in God and would not forget his deeds but would keep his commands.*

PASSING OF THE BATON

Fathers, the Bible teaches us we are called to pass our faith on to our children so that they will in turn pass their faith in Christ to their children. (If there is a young adult without a father present, please adjust accordingly.) Young adult would you please face the congregation and extend your hand behind you (as a track relay racer would do). Dads, now please reach forward and hand off the baton to your young adult. Young adults, don't look back. Please keep looking forward. There is symbolism in this. The parent continues to encourage and cheer you on as you run the race of life!

The Bible says in 3 John 4: "I have no greater joy than to hear my children are walking in the truth."

Let's give these participants a round of applause as they and their families are seated.

The participants are now going to come and share a word of testimony with you. They will come in alphabetical order.

Appendix E
ROP Testimonials

ROP is a truly remarkable and enlightening process. It takes a young person and dually reinforces and affirms their faith, both in their lives, and in the life of their church. It builds their faith up, while at the same time putting it to the test, and then sends that equipped young person out into the line of duty. The result is unlike anything I've ever seen before. It showed me that though I may not be as wise or capable as my elders, I am certainly not worthless; I am capable of serving in the body of Christ. ROP is an incredible experience, and I think it's one of the most phenomenal programs that has been introduced to the Christian church in decades.

Coleman-ROP Participant

Taking part in the Rite of Passage ceremony changed my life. It allowed me to learn for myself exactly what God calls me to be and do with my life. The experience granted me such a satisfaction in not only my life with my family and peers but also my spiritual life. It gave me the hope and belief that I was more than I ever knew. For the first time people expected me to succeed and I was held responsible for my actions. For this I am thankful. It gave me exactly the strength and desire for God that I needed in my life.

Alyssa-ROP participant

I'm really glad that I did the Rite of Passage it really helped me to share my salvation with others. I think the Rite of Passage is a great way to share your testimony with others.

Allison-ROP participant

I was so thankful that my daughter had this opportunity and acted upon it. I feel she was blessed by it, in the time she put forth to study and write about the questions. It made her look inward and voice her convictions and love for the Lord. ROP is something she can refer back to later and hopefully see growth from then to now. It also gave her the opportunity to study her heritage, claim it, and share it.

Cynthia-mother of ROP participant

The challenging and faith probing questions are an important part of ROP and they provide the structure for assessing the readiness of the young adult. It is very much a process where you get out of it what you put into it. But for me as a father the added benefit was the opportunity to mark a point in time with my son, drive a stake in the ground if you will, and acknowledge that as when he became a young man. Over the generations we have lost the importance and significance of this and now it is hard for a father to even know how to go about it. ROP really opens the door for this and helps to facilitate the father-son (or father-daughter) conversations that need to take place. Because ROP sets an anchor point, my son truly sees himself as a young man ready to step up and serve the Lord and his church in any way he can. "When I was a child, I spake as a child, I understood as a child, I thought as a child: but when I became a man, I put away childish things." 1 Cor. 13:11-KJV.

Dan-father of ROP participant

ROP was an awesome experience for me. It was challenging and I really had to put time into it. It wasn't just something that took me an hour. It took a lot of time and thought. The questions were tough and I had to look up a lot of Scripture. God really did a work in my life through this. I'm sure many people think that after we went through this process that we went back to our normal lives of being "kids," but if you were really serious about it that meant that your whole demeanor and actions changed because you were no longer a kid, you were a young adult. I am so thankful that I went through ROP. It changed my life.

Kandace-ROP Participant

We are so thankful for a pastor that values young people enough to invest the time and effort to coordinate a program like Rite of Passage. As parents, we are striving to teach our children the biblical principles they need to be in the world, yet not "of" it. Having our pastor come alongside us to reinforce the concepts we're teaching in our home has made a world of difference in "cementing" the foundation. The thought-provoking questions helped our son search himself and really "nail down a few loose ends." We're glad Pastor Kevin challenged him with hard questions. As a Christian man, he'll have to answer "hard" questions about his faith for the rest of his life. This was wonderful preparation. The letters he received as a result of ROP were such a blessing to him and the whole family. There have been a lot of times in my life when I would have loved a "word" from my grandmother after she was gone. He has a "word" from each of his grandparents, parents, siblings, uncle, etc. What a precious treasure for him in years to come!

Melanie-mother of ROP participant

Rite of Passage was such a tremendous blessing and I will never forget that precious time. For me, it was a time of summing up all I had experienced for many years of my life. My parents had trained, taught and were expecting me to act like a young adult; so when it was time for me to go through Rite of Passage, it was an easy transition. I greatly enjoyed the time I spent studying the Word of God and learning more about my grandparents and great-grandparents. The ceremony was a special day; the finishing touch. My family surrounding me with the love and prayers during the service was truly more encouraging than I can ever say. Experiencing that made me desire to be a young adult more than I had ever wanted and I immediately got involved in activities in my church, including singing in our Praise Team. Rite of Passage was the perfect prod for me to enter young adulthood and most importantly, a closer walk with Jesus.

Katy-ROP participant

Rite of Passage is a great experience. It has in-depth questions about oneself that really challenge you to examine your physical and spiritual life. There was one question that said, "If you only had two weeks left to live, what would you do?" This question showed me what my priorities are now, and what they should be. Even though this process was tough, it is a time in which you will learn many new things and reap the benefits for many years to come.

Psalm 17:5 My steps have held to your paths; my feet have not stumbled.

Josh-ROP Participant

A sincere and heart felt thank you for the opportunity and blessing of being a part of ROP. All churches should consider incorporating ROP as part of the life of their church. It is vital that we cement our young adults in Christ. ROP can help facilitate that by making them take an internal look at their salvation experience and walk with the one true God. In addition, it gives a boy or girl a point in time to mark their passage into adulthood. They will take a look at some hard questions in life concerning character and purity. This is what most churches have been missing which leaves their young adults disconnected with and therefore walking away from the doors of the church that they once entered. Raising the bar to maturity and service within the body of believers is what ROP can help accomplish. Finally, it strengthens the family by binding their hearts together through the process of sharing heart-felt letters from close family members and friends along with researched information about grand-parents and great-grandparents. It helps continue the heritage of Jesus Christ and sets them on a course to run the race for Him. Our son and whole family was blessed to participate in ROP.

Todd and Beverly-Parents of ROP Participant

Rite of Passage is one of the most unique things I have ever seen in the church. I have been through youth groups and teen oriented Sunday school classes time and again, but this experience, I felt, was much more involving. The whole process touches on basic aspects of the Christian life and forced me to look at them from a purely Biblical point of view. What touched me most deeply was not a particular question or Bible verse, but the idea behind Rite of Passage. I learned that Christians need to be actively involved in teaching their younger Christian Brothers and Sisters what God expects of them and how they should act as young adults. If the older generations simply dump the younger members of their family onto a youth pastor or small group of "specialized" leaders, then there is little connection to the church body. However, by setting expectations and standards upon young adults, children grow up to see that they are wanted and cherished by their elders, and that special connection dramatically increases their want to grow in Christ. I love how Rite of Passage encourages young adults to grow up using all the potential they possess, and it ensures us that the church is standing by our shoulder, ready to help us stand strong and catch us if we fall.

Keith-ROP Participant

For more information or if you would like to contact Kevin about coming to speak to your church or group please email him at kevin@mpbc.ws. He also has a blog at dkevinbrown.WordPress.com.

On Church Leadership

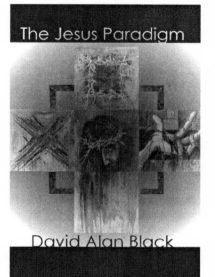

David Alan Black, author of *The Myth of Adolescence* and numerous other books, takes a look at what the church and its leadership should look like in the light of the Gospel Commission, the teachings of Jesus, and the practice of the early church.

In The Jesus Paradigm, he calls on us to change our entire way of thinking, our paradigm, move away from titles and other trappings of authority and position, and begin to live and lead as Jesus did—by sacrificing ourselves and living for others.

This book may anger you, or it may encourage you. But it will definitely challenge you.

Prepared to
Give an Answer?

Elgin Hushbeck, Jr. takes on the basics of Christianity and teaches readers how to understand and defend their faith in this volume and its companion volume, *Evidence for the Bible*. The two volumes are suitable for personal study, for groups in the church, or for homeschoolers who want a solid foundation in thinking about and defending their Christian faith.

Challenge your young adults to prepare themselves to give an answer to anyone who would challenge them, and to do so both gently and effectively (1 Pet. 3:15).

There are study guides available for each volume.

More from Energion Publications

Personal Study

The Jesus Paradigm	$17.99
Finding My Way in Christianity	$16.99
When People Speak for God	$17.99
Holy Smoke, Unholy Fire	$14.99
Not Ashamed of the Gospel	$12.99
Evidence for the Bible	$16.99
Christianity and Secularism	$16.99
What's In A Version?	$12.99
Christian Archy	$9.99
Ultimate Allegiance	$9.99
The Messiah and His Kingdom to Come	$19.99 (B&W)

Christian Living

52 Weeks of Ordinary People – Extraordinary God	$7.99
Daily Devotions of Ordinary People – Extraordinary God	$19.99
Directed Paths	$7.99
Grief: Finding the Candle of Light	$8.99
I Want to Pray	$7.99
Soup Kitchen for the Soul	$12.99

Bible Study

Learning and Living Scripture	$12.99
To the Hebrews: A Participatory Study Guide	$9.99
Revelation: A Participatory Study Guide	$9.99
The Gospel According to St. Luke: A Participatory Study Guide	$8.99
Identifying Your Gifts and Service: Small Group Edition	$12.99
Why Four Gospels?	$11.99

Theology

God's Desire for the Nations	$18.99
Operation Olive Branch	$16.99

Generous Quantity Discounts Available
Dealer Inquiries Welcome
Energion Publications
P.O. Box 841
Gonzalez, FL 32560
Website: http://energionpubs.com
Phone: (850) 525-3916

CPSIA information can be obtained at www.ICGtesting.com
Printed in the USA
BVOW040040160512

290168BV00001B/22/P